Praise for *Pagan*

"In *Paganism in Depth*, John Beckett once again builds a solid corpus from which a foundation of Paganism is derived, a practical and studied approach to practice is achieved, and in-depth understanding into next steps is described. John is thorough and insightful in his presentation: every section provides building blocks for those new to the path and those weathered in the Way. The reader will come away with knowledge, workable methods, and an understanding of the road ahead. There are treasures to be found here!"

—Rev. Jean (Drum) Pagano, Archdruid of Ár nDraíocht Féin (ADF)

"For those looking to intensify and deepen their Pagan practice, Beckett's latest offering provides an inspirational, personal, and sagacious resource to do just that. Take your Paganism to the next level with this challenging yet important and timely work."

—Kristoffer Hughes, head of the Anglesey Druid Order and author of *From the Cauldron Born* and *The Celtic Tarot*

"*Paganism in Depth* is the elusive 'next-level book' that genuinely provides a roadmap for building a deeper and more meaningful Pagan practice. Beckett provides the insight and knowledge necessary to build a lasting relationship with both deity and the people who make up the greater Pagan community. This book will strengthen your magickal practice and add fire to your spiritual work. Great reading for Druids, Witches, and anyone in the magickal world who lives in a world full of gods."

—Jason Mankey, author of *The Witch's Athame* and *The Witch's Book of Shadows*

PAGANISM
IN DEPTH

Photo by Tesa Morin

ABOUT THE AUTHOR

John Beckett grew up in Tennessee with the woods right outside his back door. Wandering through them gave him a sense of connection to nature and to a certain Forest God.

John is a Druid in the Order of Bards, Ovates and Druids, and a member of Ár nDraíocht Féin. Locally, he is a member of the Denton Covenant of Unitarian Universalist Pagans, who he served as Coordinating Officer for twelve years before stepping down from formal leadership in 2017. His blog, *Under the Ancient Oaks*, is part of the Pagan channel of the multifaith website Patheos. John has been writing, speaking, teaching, and leading public rituals since 2003. His first book, *The Path of Paganism: An Experience-Based Guide to Modern Pagan Practice,* was published by Llewellyn in 2017.

John lives in the Dallas–Fort Worth area with his wife, Cathy, and their cat, Sophie. Blogging won't pay the bills, so John earns his keep as an engineer.

FOUNDATIONS, PRACTICES & CHALLENGES
A POLYTHEIST APPROACH

PAGANISM IN DEPTH

JOHN BECKETT

AUTHOR OF *THE PATH OF PAGANISM*

Llewellyn Publications
Woodbury, Minnesota

FIRST EDITION
First Printing, 2019

Book format by Samantha Penn
Cover design by Shannon McKuhen
Editing by Laura Kurtz

Llewellyn Publications is a registered trademark of Llewellyn Worldwide Ltd.

Library of Congress Cataloging-in-Publication Data
Names: Beckett, John, author.
Title: Paganism in depth : a polytheist approach / John Beckett, author of
  The path of paganism.
Description: First Edition. | Woodbury : Llewellyn Worldwide, Ltd., 2019. |
  Includes bibliographical references.
Identifiers: LCCN 2019006102 (print) | LCCN 2019012332 (ebook) | ISBN
  9780738760681 (ebook) | ISBN 9780738760643 (alk. paper)
Subjects: LCSH: Paganism.
Classification: LCC BL432 (ebook) | LCC BL432 .B43 2019 (print) | DDC
  299/.94—dc23
LC record available at https://lccn.loc.gov/2019006102

Llewellyn Worldwide Ltd. does not participate in, endorse, or have any authority or responsibility concerning private business transactions between our authors and the public.

All mail addressed to the author is forwarded, but the publisher cannot, unless specifically instructed by the author, give out an address or phone number.

Any internet references contained in this work are current at publication time, but the publisher cannot guarantee that a specific location will continue to be maintained. Please refer to the publisher's website for links to authors' websites and other sources.

Llewellyn Publications
A Division of Llewellyn Worldwide Ltd.
2143 Wooddale Drive
Woodbury, MN 55125-2989
www.llewellyn.com

Printed in the United States of America

DEDICATION

FOR THOSE WHO SERVE their gods and their communities when it's easy and when it's hard, who take their Paganism ever deeper even when there's no map, and who trust their own senses when encountering things that some say cannot be: you are building something sacred and beautiful. This book is dedicated to you.

CONTENTS

ACKNOWLEDGMENTS

MUCH OF THE MATERIAL in this book was originally written for my blog, *Under the Ancient Oaks*. It's been organized, edited, reorganized, reedited, and then edited again. What you hold is not the result of copying and pasting text from blog to book. Rather, it's an entity all its own.

This book would not have happened without the support and inspiration of my family of choice.

To Jason Mankey, my editor at Patheos Pagan, who keeps telling me how great my writing is: I'm still not sure I believe you, but I like hearing it. I'm extremely grateful for your support, and for your dedication to the Pagan movement even when things get more difficult (and more personal) than they should.

To Chris Godwin, Amanda Godwin, and all the people who make the ADF Texas Imbolc Retreat something to look forward to every February: you show us what public polytheism can be.

To Gabrielle Milburn and Morgan Milburn: you stand as constant reminders that inexperience can be quickly overcome with consistent effort. Your dedication inspires me.

To Linda Masten: your love for your ancestors is a joy to see, and your commitment to your communities is beyond virtuous—it is heroic.

To Cynthia Talbot: you are my fellow priest and co-adventurer on this journey of depth and discovery. This book is your story as much as it is mine. I do not know if we will get there in this lifetime, but we have gone far and we will go farther, and we are leaving good notes for those who come after us.

To Cathy Beckett: this is not your path, but somehow you are always there, supporting me and those around me, no matter how strong the storms … even when the storms have real rain and wind and we're all cold and wet. I could not do this without you.

To all of you, and to all the friends, family, and co-religionists who are too numerous to list but whose support is critical: thank you.

INTRODUCTION

I STILL REMEMBER THE joy I felt when I first discovered Paganism.

I learned the Divine is feminine as well as masculine—and many, not one. Nature is sacred. Magic is real. I would later learn that none of those things are universal in Paganism, but this is what was presented to me and I liked it. Something in the core of my being had always whispered that these things wer true. Now I finally had a name to attach to it.

I loved it and wanted more. I wanted to go *deeper*.

So I went exploring. I bought books and devoured them. I collected magical tools and consecrated them. I cast spells and celebrated the turning of the seasons. I talked to as many other Pagans as I could find and asked them questions as long as they'd answer. And as I talked with them, I noticed something interesting—most of them were using the same books I was using. Paganism, it seemed, was Scott Cunningham, Silver RavenWolf, and Starhawk. They were good authors, but I already knew their books were primarily for beginners. Where were the intermediate and advanced books? Where was the deeper material?

I soon learned a few things; first, that the form of Paganism I had been introduced to was Wicca, and Paganism is more than Wicca. It's *broader* than that—there are many varieties of modern Paganism. Before I could find the deeper levels of Wicca, I found Druidry. Once again, I felt joy when I discovered a name for something I always knew was true.

I took Druidry deeper. I joined the Order of Bards, Ovates and Druids, and worked through the study materials for their three grades over a six-year period. I read books on practicing Druidry by Philip Carr-Gomm, John Michael Greer, and Isaac Bonewits. I read books on the history of Druidry by Peter Berresford Ellis and Ronald Hutton. I started going to Druid gatherings where I could compare notes with other practicing Druids and learn from them.

Again, I learned a few things. I learned that while most Druids ground their practices in a love of nature and of Celtic lore, some ground their practices in relationships with gods, ancestors, and other spiritual beings. Once again, my desire for depth led me to breadth, to different ways of seeing the world and of being a Pagan.

Around that time, I had a series of powerful firsthand ecstatic experiences of several gods. Again, I wanted to go deeper. I began to study polytheism. I read books on the origins of religion and of language. I read about the beliefs and practices of some of the world's remaining tribal societies. I rearranged my own practice and centered it on honoring the gods who were speaking to me.

This same sequence of events keeps repeating over and over again: I discover something that speaks to my soul and I want to go deeper. I explore it in more depth, consulting more specialized sources and narrowing the focus of my practice. And then I discover that this new deeper level isn't only one thing; it too has many areas of interest and focus. I can't dive deep into all of them—I have to pick one or perhaps two and dedicate myself to them, while deemphasizing others.

At each level I found people who are happy there and who aren't interested in going any deeper. Those folks who had been Wiccans for fifteen years and were still working with Scott Cunningham books (which, to be clear, are a good place to start) had all the Paganism they wanted. That's fine. Some people want to be rock guitarists, some people want season tickets to the symphony, and some people want to turn on the radio and listen to country music. None are "better" than the others. We all have to find the kind of music and the level of musical involvement that's right for us. The same is true with our religion and spirituality.

But some of us want to go as deep as we can.

My first book, *The Path of Paganism* (2017), is the story of my journey out of Christian fundamentalism and into Paganism. It shows how to build a meaningful and helpful Pagan practice based on reason and experience. It's the book I always wanted to hand to beginners when they asked me, "How do I get started?" and to intermediate Pagans when they asked, "What's next?"

This book is the story of the next steps on my Pagan path. Because it's a deeper book, it is necessarily a narrower book. This is not the only way to go deeper into Paganism, but it is how I have gone deeper.

Part 1 of *Paganism In Depth* deals with the concepts that form the foundation of a deep Pagan practice. If you're going hiking you need to be prepared, and some hikes require more preparation than others. If you're going on a ten-minute hike on a well-maintained trail, you need only be physically capable of walking there and back. For a two-mile hike on mostly level terrain, take a bottle of water and you'll be fine. But if you're hiking the Appalachian Trail—all 2,200 miles from Georgia to Maine, or a few segments of it—you need a backpack, a tent, a sleeping bag, all the food and water you can carry, and arrangements for resupply along the way. You also need to be in excellent physical condition. Want to hike for a month through unmarked territory in Alaska? You'd better have some serious wildcrafting skills, because there aren't any grocery stores to drop in along the way. And there are risks you don't see even in the wooded areas of more inhabited areas … like grizzly bears.

The comparison to deeper religious and spiritual practice isn't perfect, but the key point remains: be prepared. Doing this deeper work well requires a strong foundation in basic concepts like animism, ancestor veneration, and polytheism.

The interlude of this book is titled "I Like It Here—Why Do I Have to Leave?" Sometimes we find a certain level of skill and commitment and think we've found where we need to be for the rest of our lives. But in a year or two or ten, we start hearing a call to move on again. This section explores what that call looks, sounds, and feels like, why we might want to leave a place where we're comfortable, and how we can begin the journey.

Part 2 covers the spiritual practices that will support us on our deeper journey. Running is perhaps the simplest of sports. All you need to participate are some good shoes and a stretch of reasonably safe roads or trails. Anyone in decent health with ordinary mobility can do it. Start running a little a few times a week and before long you can be ready to complete a 5K race. Add more miles and more consistency and within a year or so you can complete a marathon. In 2016, more than a half million people finished a marathon in the United States. But if you want to run in the Olympic marathon, you're going to need a different level of training (and some natural talent, but that's another matter). You're going to have to run a hundred miles or more every week, including hills, sprints, and long runs. You'll need a detailed stretching program, massages, and ice treatments. And you'll need to eat a very careful diet to make sure you have enough calories to fuel intense levels of exercise while keeping your body weight at its optimum level. Running is running, but running at the Olympic level is very different from running for fun.

Likewise, if you just want to honor your gods and live in harmony with nature, that requires one level of practice. But if you want to experience those gods first-hand and embody their virtues in your life, if you want to work effective magic in a religious context, and if you want to take your Paganism as deep as you can, you're going to need a different level and intensity of practice. This section will cover devotion, magic, divination, and ecstatic practice.

Part 3 covers the challenges we encounter when we begin practicing more deeply. I remember the summer I moved into my first apartment. I got my furniture set up and stocked the kitchen. I thought I was done. Then I went into the bathroom and realized there was no toilet paper and no shower curtain. I knew toilet paper wasn't supplied with an apartment, but I was used to someone else buying it. And I really had no idea I had to supply my own shower curtain. Years later, my wife and I moved into our first house. When the roof suddenly started leaking, I couldn't just call the landlord and tell him to get it fixed. I *was* the landlord; I had to take care of it myself. Other things came up that I never expected: A burned-out light bulb in a fixture that wouldn't open. Termites in the door frame. Cracks in the foundation. Home ownership is an adventure, to say the least.

Again, the comparison isn't perfect, but it illustrates how when you move deeper into something, all of a sudden you have to deal with new challenges. Some of them you probably should have expected, while others would have never occurred to you until you encountered them. What do you do when you experience something in your spiritual practice that defies explanation? What do you do when your gods are demanding? What do you do when doubts start to creep into your practice? I don't have all the answers, but I can tell you what I've done and what I've seen other people do in similar situations.

ANCESTRAL, DEVOTIONAL, ECSTATIC, ORACULAR, MAGICAL, PUBLIC, PAGAN POLYTHEISM

That's a mouthful, isn't it? But if we're going to go deeper, we need to begin with a very important question: deeper into what? This is where my journey has taken me up to this point. This is the religion I practice. Your journey will likely take you somewhere different—perhaps slightly different, perhaps very different. But the methods and processes presented in this book will help you find your way regardless of the direction you take and what your deep Paganism does or doesn't include.

Some polytheists do not practice magic. They believe it is impious—that it attempts to claim for ourselves what belongs only to the gods. I do practice it because my polytheism comes out of the modern Pagan traditions that emphasize magic, so you'll find lots on magic in this book. Some polytheists practice animal sacrifice. There are very few, but for those who do, it is a religiously meaningful part of their traditions. I don't because animal sacrifice isn't part of my practice, so you won't find it in this book.

This is the context for *Paganism In Depth*.

POLYTHEISM

The noun in that long list is polytheism—all the other words are modifiers. I lean heavily on the Anomalous Thracian's definition of polytheism: "the religious regard for many real gods." Or as I sometimes put it, the gods are real, distinct, individual persons with their own sovereignty and agency. Most importantly, this means the existence of the gods is not dependent on human thought and activity.

ANCESTRAL

All of us have a debt of honor to those who came before us. Because of them, we have life. Because of them, we have knowledge, culture, and infrastructure. At the least, we owe them our devotion. Beyond that, our ancestors are usually our most accessible spiritual allies. A Heathen saying goes, "If you feel a tap on your shoulder, it's probably your grandfather, not the Allfather." Gods and spirits are often busy, and your goals may not line up with their goals. But our ancestors want to see their lines survive and succeed. Building and maintaining relationships with ancestors of blood and of spirit is a key component of the religion I practice.

DEVOTIONAL

It's not enough to acknowledge the existence of many gods and spirits. I also honor them with devotion. For me, this means prayer, meditation, and offerings. I speak to them, listen for them, and attempt to make them welcome with offerings of food and drink, and occasionally other things. The gods know they're gods; they don't need us to remind them of that. We, on the other hand, frequently need to be reminded that they're gods and we aren't.

ECSTATIC

Although the religion I practice is a reasonable religion, it is first and foremost a religion grounded in experience—the firsthand experience of gods and spirits. Sometimes this experience is an inaudible voice or a thought you know isn't yours. Sometimes it's the intimate presence of a divine being. And sometimes a god takes over your body and if you're lucky, you get to see it even if you can't do anything to stop it.

Religious ecstasy can be addictive, but these are sacred experiences, not amusement park rides. Remember also that they're UPG (unverified personal gnosis.) They may be authoritative for you, but you can't expect someone else to take your word for what a god wants them to do unless they choose to do so (personally speaking, I have on numerous occasions.) When some people tell me that a god spoke to them, I smile and nod. When people I know and respect tell me the same thing, I sit up and pay attention. Figure out who you trust and which messages strike you as authentic and which don't.

ORACULAR

My tradition is an oracular tradition: the gods speak to us. Sometimes they speak to us in ecstatic experiences as described above. Other times they speak in omens and auguries. Reading omens and auguries in the natural world requires a familiarity with nature. Sometimes a crow is a message from the Morrigan, but most times it's just a crow doing crow things. Got a question and you're not hearing or seeing anything? Ask! Use your favorite divination system. As the word origin implies, divination comes from the divine.

It is rare that the gods speak to say, "Hi, I really am here" or, "Just wanted you to know you're doing a great job." Most times they speak to call us to action or warn us of something that requires our attention … though those warnings are rarely as specific as we'd like. Sometimes people are oracles and are given a message to relay to others. I've had that responsibility a few times, and occasionally those messages were unpleasant to deliver. But I relayed them, and so far no one's tried to shoot the messenger.

MAGICAL

Most of us know the Old Testament forbids witchcraft, as did the Roman Empire because they feared its malevolent use. However, laws rarely stopped anyone from working magic in ancient times, and it rarely stops anyone today if their need is great enough. If I kept anything from my early explorations of Wicca, it's the idea that magic is our legacy and our right. It may be stealing fire from the gods, but it's also part of learning and growing and taking responsibility for our own lives. There is no particular form of magic tied to my religion. I tend to be rather utilitarian about magic; if a technique works, I'll use it.

PUBLIC

My religion is not for the few, the skilled, or the special. It's for anyone and everyone who wants to be a part of it. Part of my calling is to facilitate public rituals for anyone with any degree of interest and commitment. I'm called to be a priest for the plumber and the accountant as much as for the seer and the witch.

Not everything I do is for public consumption. I'm not really concerned about scaring people and giving them a bad impression of Paganism, but I am concerned with the sanctity of the mysteries. I don't do ecstatic possession in public ritual; most people wouldn't understand it and would walk away with the wrong idea about what they saw.

I want everyone to go as far and as deep as their skills, interests, and willingness to work will take them. While it's unreasonable to expect everyone to be a priest, it's also unreasonable to hold back some people because others are unable or unwilling to do what's necessary to go deeper.

If you're reading this book, there's some part of you that wants to go deeper, even if you're not sure what that means ... even if it scares you a little *or* if it scares you a lot.

PAGAN

Some polytheists make a big deal of saying, "I'm a polytheist, not a Pagan." Some like to point out that their tradition did not originate in the Pagan revival that began in the late nineteenth century. Mine did, with a lineage that runs through Scott Cunningham and Margot Adler. It runs through Isaac Bonewits and Ross Nichols. It runs through Gerald Gardner and Aleister Crowley. I've moved away from the teachings of most of those ancestors, but I would not be where I am today without them. I am a polytheist above all, but the polytheist religion I practice is firmly and proudly inside the Big Tent of Paganism.

So, why am I an ancestral, devotional, ecstatic, oracular, magical, public, Pagan polytheist? Because this is where my journey led me. At each step, I held on to what was meaningful and helpful, and I discarded what didn't work. This is what the gods continue to call me to do and be. All these elements are coming together to form one tradition I practice, explore, and teach to others, even if it takes a lot of words to describe it.

This is not the only way to practice Paganism, and it is not the only way to practice polytheism. However, it is a way that works well for me and others. Will it work for you? The only way to know for sure is to try it and see for yourself.

PART 1:
FOUNDATIONS

1

SEEING THE WORLD IN A DIFFERENT WAY

We all have assumptions in our lives, things we've always been told are true that we don't question. Many times, we don't recognize these statements as assumptions—they're just the way things are.

In 2004, the Red River Unitarian Universalist Church was founded in Denison, Texas. Like all churches in the state, they filed papers with the Texas state comptroller for tax-exempt status. Their application was rejected. The comptroller said they had no sacred text, no unifying belief, and no belief in a higher power—obviously, they weren't a real religion. In her explanation, she said, "We have to have rules, or anybody can claim tax-exempt status." That may be true, but whose rules are we playing by? A couple of phone calls from the UUA headquarters cleared that up, but it showed some of the assumptions people make about religion in our wider society.

A few years ago, I was describing Paganism to someone who was completely unfamiliar with it. I talked about the Divine as both female and male, ancient ancestors and their beliefs and practices, and forming a connection with the Earth and with her rhythms and cycles. When I was done, this person said, "Well, what I really want to know is how does Paganism say you get to heaven?"

My answer was, "That's not a relevant question in Paganism." As a Pagan, my religion is about honoring the gods and ancestors, living in harmony with the Earth and all her creatures, and living in such a way that when I leave this world and join the ancestors, I will be worthy of the honor of those who come after me. The afterlife will take care of itself.

This is another assumption—that all religions must be about what happens after you die, and ensuring you end up in the good place and not the bad place. But what if there is no good place or bad place, just an Otherworld much like this one? Perhaps we'll be reincarnated back into this world. Perhaps there's only this one life. Or perhaps there's something else none of us have even thought of.

You may be familiar with Pascal's Wager. Seventeenth-century mathematician and philosopher Blaise Pascal argued that a rational person should believe in the Christian god even if they aren't sure he exists. Believe in God and if there is a God, you go to heaven; if there isn't, you get nothing. But if you don't believe, you get nothing if you're right and end up in hell if you're wrong. Clearly the rational choice is to believe in God.

There's a cartoon I see on Facebook from time to time. A priest, rabbi, and imam are walking down the street debating religion and not paying attention to traffic. They wander into the street, get hit by a truck, and all three are killed. They begin to float upward, and one of them turns to the others and says, "At least now we'll finally find out who's right." They come not to pearly gates but to a great hall. And there they see an old man wearing an eye patch, with two ravens sitting on his shoulder and a sign that says "Odin."

Pascal's Wager makes the bad assumption that there are only two options: either the Christian god exists, or there are no gods at all. It also assumes that if the Christian god exists, he will send nonbelievers to hell, a belief that Christian Universalists and many others reject.

This is the environment in which we work. Like fish who aren't aware of the water in which they swim, even the most mindful of us often don't see all the Christian and materialistic concepts that influence our thinking and our lives. Many of us come to Paganism from other religions. It follows that if we simply start our new religion where we left off with our old one and don't do any work to examine our assumptions, our new religion and new spirituality will be built on the foundation of our mainstream society … and that's a recipe for failure. Most people never examine their unstated (and in some cases, unconscious) assumptions. They retain the foundational assumptions, philosophy, and the religious methods of the religion of their childhood or the religion of the mainstream society.

I was thrilled to become a Pagan at age 31, but my practice floundered for eight years because I wasn't dealing with the foundational assumptions of my fundamentalist Christian upbringing and of the mainstream culture. It was only when I committed to examine these assumptions and to build a new foundation that I was able to become the kind of Pagan I wanted to be. There is something else, something better, something that works—we just have to do the work to adopt it. We have to learn to see the world in a different way.

FACTS AND REASON— AVOIDING MATERIALIST ASSUMPTIONS

Let's begin with our assumptions about something very important and very basic: facts and reason.

Our mainstream society has problems with facts and reason. Some of this is due to intellectual laziness, some is for political expediency, and some is because of unstated and unexamined assumptions. It's important for us to clear up these errors and misunderstandings not so we can win arguments but so the Pagan beliefs and practices that are so important to us will be built on a firm foundation of both experience and reason. Our deepest responses to the big questions of life need to be grounded in reality. But the question of what constitutes reality is often confused by unstated materialist assumptions—not facts.

Materialism is not consumerism. Materialism is the philosophical assumption that all that exists is matter and the products of its interactions. It reduces human experiences of love and beauty to the interactions of brain chemistry. It assumes that gods and spirits not only do not exist but they *cannot* exist. A few scientists argue that quantum physics disproves materialism. I'm not sure it does, and in any case I'm very uncomfortable invoking quantum physics to "prove" anything. But whether it does or doesn't, materialism remains an assumption of science (or rather, of many scientists), not a finding *of* science.

So when someone says, "there's no way magic could work" what they're *really* saying is, "there's no way magic could work in a materialist universe." Magic could work by the intercession of gods and spirits, but materialism refuses to consider that possibility. It says there is no evidence but excludes non-material evidence. All the times magic does work are dismissed as coincidences and confirmation bias because the evidence points toward conclusions that invalidate their materialist assumptions and they refuse to question them. That isn't science—it's claiming science proves something when it doesn't.

Materialism need not lead to nihilism. Naturalists, humanists, and other nontheists take the assumptions of materialism and say, "yes, and life is still beautiful and meaningful." That's a valid spiritual path, and for some, the only spiritual path they can embrace with integrity. But like all religious and philosophical paths, it's based on foundational assumptions that are ultimately unprovable.

Begin by separating facts from interpretation. Some materialists like to say our religious, spiritual, and magical experiences aren't real. Those people are absolutely wrong—these experiences are undeniably, unquestionably real. It is our interpretations of these experiences that are open to debate. Unfortunately, some people can't seem to separate facts from their interpretations of the facts.

In June of 2016, I saw a green glowing bird. It was something that many people say cannot exist, but there it was.

Let me be as precise and as non-presumptive as I can: I saw something that looked and acted like a bird. It was green and glowing in a way that living, this-world creatures just don't do. It was in a place where there are no native birds that are green, and it was with a large group of other birds that appeared to be of the same species, except they weren't green. A skeptical commenter on my blog listed a variety of materialist explanations for this experience (and did so respectfully, which I appreciate). I described why each explanation didn't fit, and why an Otherworldly explanation makes the most sense to me.

That I saw something is a fact. My interpretation of it is an opinion about which reasonable people can have reasonable disagreements. But reasonable disagreements should only be around the interpretation, not around the facts of the experience. Too often we do this to ourselves. We have a religious or magical experience and are unable to come up with a "proper" materialist explanation for it, so we start to tell ourselves it wasn't real. It didn't really happen. We gaslight ourselves. Or we stand by as others do it to us.

Our experiences are real. Let's explore all possible interpretations, and if the facts lead us to an ordinary, this-world explanation, so be it. Sometimes a mysterious light in the middle of the night is just a neighbor playing with a flashlight ... and sometimes it isn't.

Reason and reasoning are a process—materialism is an assumption. My experience of the green glowing bird was the effect. What was the cause? I eliminated the skeptical explanations because none of them fit. I considered reports of similar experiences from other people who I trust to relay them accurately. I considered the lore of our ancestors, who weren't so caught up in looking "educated" and "sophisticated" as we are. I considered other, similar experiences of my own. That line of reasoning led me to conclude (tentatively, since we can never be absolutely sure about such things) that either this was an Otherworldly bird that had made its way into our world, or that a bird from this world had wandered into one of those mysterious places where this world and the Otherworld intersect.

A skeptic can argue that one of the possibilities I rejected is a more likely cause. They might be right. But to argue that there is no reasoning in that assessment is to argue that reason and materialism are the same things, and they are not.

I can't prove the gods are real. I can prove that my life is better (more meaningful and less fearful, though certainly no easier) since I began this Pagan journey. It is a very reasonable (i.e., properly connecting cause and effect) thing for me to be a Pagan, even if I can't convince skeptics of the absolute truth of my beliefs and practices.

Evidence is more than double-blind, peer reviewed studies. I have to laugh when I see people claiming there's no evidence that magic works. If you want to see evidence for magic, then practice magic. Magic doesn't work on belief, it works on action. Do the spells and you'll get results. You also have to do the spells right—waving a wand like a mad symphony conductor isn't going to accomplish anything. Understand that magic doesn't make things happen; it increases the odds that things will happen. It is possible to do everything right and still not get the result you expect. Working magic once or twice isn't going to prove anything to anyone, but over time the results will start to add up. Eventually the results will be impossible to ignore. And at that point, it would be easier to accept that magic is real than to continue with denials and rationalizations. The same thing is true for first-hand experiences of gods and spirits. Once might be a coincidence and twice might be self-delusion, but as experiences start to stack up, it gets harder and harder to come to any conclusion other than they're as real as real can get.

We are not free to believe anything we like. Some things are demonstrably false. Others are so unlikely they're not worth our time and effort. But in the realm of religion and spirituality, much is uncertain. The choice of what religion to follow and how to follow it is deeply personal. Each of us must make our own decisions, and we must make them based on the standards of evidence that make sense to us. I have Pagan friends who happily practice magic but who find insufficient evidence for the existence of many real gods. I have other Pagan friends who join me in the worship of the gods but who find magic implausible. Their beliefs are no less reasonable because they are different. And if someone really and truly believes their materialist assumptions, that is also a reasonable approach and one I respect even if I don't share it. That said, facts and reason are not exclusive to materialism. Our deep Pagan experiences and practices can be reasonable (and *must* be reasonable, I would argue) even if those who are locked into a materialist worldview won't accept them.

ANIMISM

We need a philosophical alternative to materialism. Thankfully, we don't have to invent it. A good alternative already exists: animism.

Do you talk to your cat? Of course you do. I don't know a single cat owner—excuse me, a person who is owned by cats—who doesn't talk to their feline friends. I'm not a dog person, but I see the same behavior from them. Why do we do this? Even small children realize animals can't understand language. But our intuition tells us we can communicate with them. And so we do, even if all they hear is voice tone and body language.

Do you talk to trees? It's not as common as talking to animals, but if you're any sort of nature-centered Pagan, you've probably done it. You asked permission before taking a tree branch to make a wand or before harvesting an herb that grows in your back yard. Every so often I see an article that recommends talking to your house plants. They usually try to explain it away in materialist terms, but those of us who've done it regularly know there's something more involved.

That something more is personhood. We intuitively recognize something of ourselves in cats and dogs, in plants and trees, and if we're paying really close attention, in mountains and rivers. These aren't things, they're persons. They have inherent value and worth that does not depend on their usefulness or desirability to humans. Whatever animates us also animates cats and dogs, trees and rocks, rivers and storms. Whatever inherent sovereignty we possess, every other creature, ecosystem, and natural force also possesses. Animism is grounded in the agency of persons in the ability of a bird to fly where birds want to fly; in the ability of a tree to grow in the way an oak or a pine or a birch wants to grow. Animism is also grounded in our choice to relate to birds and trees respectfully as persons and not things. Whether your dog has a soul or not doesn't affect how you relate to your dog. This line of thinking is intuitive even to us here in the west in the twenty-first century.

In her book *The Wakeful World*, Emma Restall Orr gives a more sophisticated definition of animism that states everything has mind and that mind and matter are not separate. She says we can never see the world as it actually is but only our idea of it. Our ideas are then "data processed through the filters of perception established by beliefs based on limitations and experience." We don't see the personhood of cats and trees and lakes because the mainstream religion tells us we alone were made "in the image of God," and we like being in the top position. It lets us justify exploiting other persons for our own greed.

Are all these persons (including ourselves) inhabited by spirits? Are all these persons spirits who are currently manifesting in a physical form? Or are the spirit and the form inseparable elements of one whole person? I don't know. My intuition tells me everything is inspirited; it does not tell me the structure of the spirits involved.

If you don't hear much about animism, it's because early anthropologists and the school texts based from their work called it primitive. They presented a model of so-called progress that went from superstition to animism to polytheism to monotheism to proper Protestant Christianity. In the last fifty years or so, that model has been extended to make atheism the pinnacle of human progress. We like to think of ourselves as advanced and those who came before us as primitive—the idea that our ancient ancestors' thinking might be more accurate and more helpful never occurs to us.

But we still talk to our cats.

If every other creature, ecosystem, and natural force is a person, can we communicate with them? Should we communicate with them? Yes, but...

Would you go up to a random person on the street and say, "What do you have to teach me?" Of course you wouldn't (or at least, I hope you wouldn't). Then why would you go up to a random tree or bird and ask the same question? If you don't think a random person on the street has some message for you, don't assume a random bird or tree does either.

Would you go up to a Buddhist monk on the street and say, "What do you have to teach me?" You might. It would be rude and presumptive, and he might teach you not to act so entitled in a way you wouldn't particularly like, but at least there's reason to believe a monk might actually be willing and able to teach you something useful. Now, if you bought the monk a cup of tea and sat with him while he drank it, he might be inclined to teach you something more in line with what you had in mind. If you started attending meditation and dharma lessons at his temple, you'd probably learn a lot more. You might even develop a friendship with the monk.

You can learn a lot from a bird or a tree, but it works best when you're in a respectful and reciprocal relationship with them. If they're persons—and they are—then treat them like persons, not like things.

The same intuition that tells us we can find a person in a cat or a tree or a mountain will also tell us we can find a person (or many persons) in our dreams, our devotions, our divination, and our worship. Whatever else the gods may be, they are also persons. And just as we would not go up to a random person on the street and ask them to teach us something or give us something, neither should we approach a random deity and ask them to fix our problems or lead us to enlightenment. As with people, our interactions with the gods work best in a respectful, reciprocal relationship.

Animism provides a framework for an inspirited and enchanted world, a world where everything you see and touch and feel and sense is not a thing, but a person worthy of your respect and capable of entering into a reciprocal relationship with you—if that person so chooses. Those persons include the gods. Animism teaches that just as I don't relate to a cat or a tree in exactly the same way as I relate to another human, I may need to relate to gods in different ways as well. Animism serves as a constant reminder to respect the dignity and sovereignty of all persons, whether they are human or not.

A MAGICAL UNIVERSE

We don't live in a materialist universe—we live in a magical universe that is stranger than we can imagine. Yes, there's a logical answer for everything, but that logic is not simple and straightforward. There are some things science can't explain yet, and other things science may never be able to explain, a fact that bothers some people. Their irritation is understandable; when foundational assumptions about the nature of the world and how it works are questioned, most people push back. So, I respect my atheist and agnostic friends and neighbors and have neither the need nor the desire to convert them. And since you're reading this book, I imagine the idea of a magical universe appeals to you too … that's a good thing, because you're living in one.

What is a magical universe?

Every living thing in the world is not a thing but a person, a person with a spirit. Our ancestors live among us. That they live on in our dreams and memories is beyond question; that they occasionally speak to us from the Otherworld is clear to those of us who've experienced them. Gods are the mightiest of spirits. I'm not exactly sure what they are beyond that. I do know they are older, stronger, and wiser than me and you. I find them worthy of worship; working with and for them have been some of the most amazing experiences of my life.

The world is probabilistic, not deterministic. Einstein famously said, "God does not play dice." Stephen Hawking responded, "Not only does God play dice, sometimes he throws them where they can't be seen." In a probabilistic universe, anything is possible. But some things are so likely they're practically certain, while other things are so unlikely they're practically impossible. Because the world is probabilistic, there is always hope, and the more we do to move the odds in our favor, the more likely we are to get a favorable outcome.

We can (at least occasionally) work wonders. The best way to believe in magic is to work magic. Magic doesn't work on belief, it works on action. Do the spell properly and you'll get results. Of course, there may also be side effects and blowback. I do not believe in the Wiccan Law of Threes (what you send out returns to you three-fold), but I do believe in what John Michael Greer calls "the strawberry jam effect"— you can't work with it without getting it all over yourself. So be mindful what you work magic for, but if you work magic you'll get results. If you expect to see bluestones flying from Wales to the Salisbury plain (one early theory for how Merlin supposedly built Stonehenge), you're likely to be disappointed. But if you have a great need, you never know which action will put you over the line from failure to success. Use all the tools at your disposal, including your magical tools.

The universe may be magical but the laws of physics still apply. Humans cannot fly without mechanical assistance. We cannot breathe underwater unless we bring air with us. We cannot see in a cave unless we bring light. These are hard limits. There are also soft limits, things that are possible separately but impossible together. I can go to the gym in the morning or I can sleep in, but I cannot do both. When I attend Pagan conventions, inevitably I miss a speaker I want to hear because I'm scheduled to speak in the same time slot. I once had a boss whose stock line about projects was "good, fast, and cheap—pick any two."

Work is still necessary. There's a reason why no human society ever went back to hunting and gathering after taking up agriculture—the food supply is greater and more certain. But it requires work. Magic will help crops to grow, but if you don't plant seeds in the ground, your harvest is guaranteed to be nothing. There are serious issues with our socio-economic system—that topic is beyond the scope of this book. But whether the economy is based on capitalism, socialism, communism, or anything else, someone still has to plant and harvest the crops. Someone still has to bake the bread. Someone still has to take out the trash. Work is still necessary. And like any other skill, magic requires practice. Lots of practice. Magic is a different kind of work, but it's still work. Necessary work.

The benefits of living in a magical universe begin with a shift to long term thinking. Yes, I know—if your house is on fire you're all about short term thinking, and rightly so. But most of our houses aren't on fire. We live in a society where all that matters is making this month's rent or impressing Wall Street with this quarter's earnings report. In contrast, our gods have the perspective of millennia. The spirits of the land were here long before we arrived and will be here long after we're gone. Our ancestors remind us there are things of value in the past and that someday we will be the ancestors. What kind of world will we leave for those who come after us? Will we be worthy of their honor? When we realize we live in a magical universe, we start to make time out of our daily urgencies to do something to make tomorrow better than today. Do that consistently and at some point, you'll look back and realize you did make your life a lot better than it used to be.

Both the consistent practice of magic and consistent religious devotion have a clarifying effect on priorities. You start to realize that once you have what you need, your time is better spent nurturing your relationships, not chasing more stuff… and you don't need a Mercedes. You may be surprised with just how little stuff you really do need… and you begin to value your relationships more and more. Build strong enough relationships and you build families of blood or of choice—people who will stand by you year after year, because they know you'll stand by them. Some of our families are living humans. Some are ancestors. Some are gods. Relationships bring the lasting comfort and security that things cannot.

There is less fear in a magical universe. When you realize the world is full of magic and you have access to it, what do you have to fear? Death? Just a transition into the next life. Hardship? Your ancestors survived far worse. Difficult circumstances? You have tools and skills to move the odds in your favor.

We should never be so arrogant as to assume the gods are on our side, but when they call us to their service and we accept, we are on their side. That doesn't mean they will make our lives easier (they usually make things harder) but it does mean someone with divine perspective believes in us. If the Forest God or the Battle Raven thinks I can do their work, my fear is misplaced.

There are some very powerful people in some very high places with a vested interest in keeping you away from magic, even if they don't believe in it themselves. They want you focused on what they're trying to sell you today. They want you to ignore your relationships and buy more stuff. They want to keep you afraid. I'm not interested in overthrowing them. I've been called to be many things—a savior isn't one of them. Instead, I'm interested in making them irrelevant in my life, and in the lives of as many people as possible. And because we live in a magical universe, I can.

And so can you.

A MODEL OF HOW THE WORLD WORKS

Every religion has a model for the way the world works, a framework for understanding life and for figuring out our place in it.

To build a house, you begin by laying a foundation. From the foundation you frame the walls, build the roof, and install siding on the outside. You install plumbing, wiring, and insulation, then add the interior walls. At that point it starts to look like a house; you can walk around and figure out if you're in the kitchen or in the bedroom. Next you add flooring, appliances, lighting, and bathroom fixtures. Eventually you move in and add your furniture and decorations, at which point you have a complete house.

Think of building a religion or a religious practice like building a house. When we start to go deeper into our Paganism, we don't yet have a "house," we have only the vaguest idea of what our practice should look and feel like. When we have religious experiences (mild or earth-shattering), we have little idea what they mean. We need context or a model of how the world works.

My "house"—that is, my model of Paganism—begins with a foundation of animism and magic. We build a framework of practices: ancestor veneration, prayer, meditation, and offerings. The roof is composed of values and virtues: hospitality, reciprocity, compassion, and justice. Our beliefs form the walls, and our customs are the decorations.

You can use the model you were taught as a child, or you borrow someone else's model. I prefer to build my own model, but don't think you have to build alone. All of us start with our foundations. Our experiences lead to belief, as we try to interpret what happened to us. Our beliefs lead to practice as we try to implement our understanding, and as we try to re-create our experiences. Practice leads to more experience. This becomes a virtuous circle that draws us into deeper understanding, deeper practice, and stronger experiences.

We don't build our models in a vacuum; we build from our own experiences. We build from the stories of our ancestors. We build from what history, archaeology, and anthropology tell us about our ancestors. We build from the experience of our co-religionists. And we build with input from science.

We build a model for the way the world works, not a once-and-for-all Grand Theory of Everything, but a continuously updated living model that provides context for our experiences—a model that is always open to new input and new interpretation.

EVALUATING YOUR MODEL

Is your model any good? How do you evaluate its new ideas and new elements? What's needed is a framework for discernment.

Our first question should be "Does it work?" Remember that just because you can't explain something in "rational" terms doesn't mean it's not true. I like to speculate and theorize as much as any engineer who wants to know how it all works, but at some point you have to put down the scalpel and enjoy the golden eggs...and don't forget to feed the goose. If it works, it's good.

Does your model conform with known facts? We have little patience with those who deny the science of evolution, the age of the Earth, and the reality of climate change just because it doesn't fit their religious texts. Let's also be careful, however, not to assume science tells us something it doesn't. Bad science makes bad religion.

Does your model make your life better? Does it help you wrestle with life's big questions? If a belief in an afterlife dissolves your fear of death, that's a good thing. If it makes you fear ending up in the wrong place, it's not.

Does your model help you understand how to live here and now? Does it motivate you to honor the past, to live in the present, and to build for the future? Does it promote strong connections and respectful reciprocal relationships?

If so, you've got a good model. If not, keep working on it.

Some things are not part of discernment. Is it easy? This doesn't really matter; good things are often hard. Is it black and white? Again, this doesn't matter. Life is complicated, so trying to pretend things are simple when they're not leads to trouble. Does it conform to your ideas about the way things ought to be? There are many things about the world I think are unfair, and denying their reality isn't helpful ... working to change them is.

We all build our lives on foundational assumptions: things we've always been told are true, things we believe are true, and sometimes things we wish were true. Many of them are not actually true but unless we question them, they will be invisible impediments to spiritual growth. Many of the mainstream culture's assumptions come from a form of Christianity that is in conflict with our values as Pagans and polytheists. Others come from political biases that sound good (to some) but are at odds with the evidence.

Examine your assumptions. Remember that they're assumptions, not facts—you can't be sure if they're true or not. That said, take note of what is likely, and what probably isn't. More importantly, what is helpful, and what causes unnecessary pain and suffering in your life? What do you want to reinforce? What do you want to change?

Now you have a foundation for your deeper exploration of Paganism. Now you have a model to help you understand the world and your place in it.

We'll talk about some of the things that go into your model in the next two chapters.

THE BENEFITS OF MUNDANE STUDIES

If Jews, Christians, and Muslims are the People of the Book, Pagans are the People of the Library. On one level this means we have many sources, not one sacred text. But on a deeper level, it's a reminder that good religion isn't just proverbs to be memorized or rules to be obeyed—it's who we are, what we are, and whose we are. Perhaps surface-level Paganism can be something we turn on when the moon is full and turn off the rest of the month, but deep Paganism is something we live day in and day out. That means it has roots not just in theology but in all the arts and sciences. There is much we can learn from mainstream scholarship.

There is one caveat to this approach. The vast majority of academic resources are written from a nontheistic and materialistic viewpoint. If you're not sure what this means, go back and read "Facts and Reason: Avoiding Materialist Assumptions" again. Let the experts tell you the facts, but *you* should decide what they mean.

Most of our Pagan traditions have roots in the beliefs and practices of our ancient ancestors, so start by reading history. Who were the Celts, or the Greeks, or the Egyptians? Where did they come from? How did their culture arise? How did it change over time? Remember: the last pharaoh of Egypt is closer in time to us than to the first pharaoh by a thousand years. While ancient cultures did not change at the rate ours is changing, none of them were fixed, particularly those which lasted for centuries.

As well, don't ignore more recent history. As Welsh Druid Kristoffer Hughes likes to say, "We're still here." The ancestral religion of the Welsh has been affected by the Romans and the English, and by the domination of Christianity. But the stories are still there, the language is still there, and perhaps most importantly, the land is still there.

History requires records, which are hard to come by in eras before writing. Archaeology and anthropology can tell us some things about how our ancient ancestors lived. It can't give us definitive answers: was Venus of Willendorf (from about 30,000 years ago) a devotional statue of a mother goddess, a self-portrait of a woman, or a child's toy? We don't know. But these studies can give us evidence from which we can draw our own conclusions.

Study languages. A different language isn't just a different set of words, it's a different grammar, different idioms, and ultimately a different way of thinking. Learning languages allows you to read source materials for yourself rather than rely on translators who may have biases very different from your own. Learning a new language (whether living or dead—Old Irish is not the same as Modern Irish) is a major commitment. I personally haven't done it; I've put my study time elsewhere. But there is no better way to get into the heads of writers than to learn their language.

Religious studies is a field many Pagans overlook. This is the systematic study of religion: what people believe, what they practice, and why. The field attempts to make its observations objectively, but "objectively" often incorrectly assumes "nontheistically." Still, the facts and theories that come out of religious studies can help us understand our own religion and the religions of others. As with other disciplines, we can use the expertise of religious scholars to find the facts we'd otherwise miss and then use our own perspective and judgement to figure out what they mean.

Though this is a book of deity-centered Paganism (not nature-centered Paganism), there is still much we can learn from biology, chemistry, physics, and other "hard sciences." Where were the stars when Göbekli Tepe was first built? Where did melting glaciers at the beginning of the current interglacial period cause sudden and catastrophic flooding, and lead to the creation of flood myths? How do the societies of our closest primate relatives differ from ours, and what does that mean for our understanding of the prehuman ancestors we all share?

As always, beware of assuming science "proves" something just because there's evidence that supports it, and be especially leery of anyone who invokes quantum physics, which is a highly technical field that few outsiders understand. And be wary of making science the final arbiter of what is and isn't true. Science does a great job of finding facts but is poorly equipped to tell us what those facts mean in our lives.

Science helps us understand the world in which we live and the world in which our ancestors lived. It provides context for our deepest beliefs and practices. When I look at the most influential books on my shelf, I see science books right alongside books of history and religion. If you're looking for advanced Pagan books, look outside the Pagan section of the bookstore.

2

PAGAN FOUNDATIONS

ANIMISM IS PERHAPS THE most basic foundation of deeper Paganism. To use a computer metaphor, it's the operating system. (Whether animism is MacOS and materialism is Windows or vice versa is a question we will not be exploring!) Note that a computer is much more than its operating system—it's also the higher-level software, the programs and applications we use to work and play on the machine. Paganism has its higher level "programs" as well; the experiences and concepts we need to do something with our religion, whether "doing something" is religious devotion or simply dealing with ordinary life. This chapter explores some of those second level foundations.

RELIGIOUS EXPERIENCE

Some religions use their sacred text as their most important foundation. But every sacred text you read is the result of someone else's religious experience. Muhammad was visited by an angel. The Buddha sat under the Bodhi tree. Their experiences and their thoughts about them were recorded in writing (sometimes long after the fact—something those who would read sacred texts literally often ignore) for those who came after them. This was mostly a good thing—there is much we can learn from other people's religious experiences. But there is also much we can learn from our own.

Religious experiences happen all the time. Most are small, so we don't notice them. We experience wonder and awe at the immensities of nature: a sunset, a mountain, the ocean, a storm. There's the miracle of birth and the transition of death. We're more likely to notice things that are out of the ordinary: animals behaving in unusual ways, knowing things we have no way of knowing, the overwhelming feeling that an ancestor or other spiritual being is nearby, coincidences that defy the laws of probability. These experiences are undeniably real. The debate is over the interpretation. What exactly just happened? And most importantly, what does it mean?

There is a great lack of understanding of religious experience in contemporary Western society, which is not particularly surprising. Religious experiences are messy, subjective, and don't play by the rules of orthodoxy—they're hard for religious leaders to control. For at least the past five hundred years, Christianity has been dominated by a very intellectual approach to religion. For Protestants, this has been *sola scriptura*, the primacy of the Bible. Catholics have done a better job of holding on to firsthand experience but are still dominated by doctrines, canon laws, and papal encyclicals. Even Evangelicals, who emphasize "conversion experiences" and personal relationships with Jesus are clear that such experiences must occur within approved boundaries and must be interpreted in approved ways. Those that vary even a bit from orthodoxy are suspected of being a "counterfeit of the devil."

Meanwhile, we have a never-ending supply of materialist killjoys who are happy to tell us that the sun is nothing more than a ball of burning hydrogen gas and that magical feeling you get when you stand under the full moon is just a product of your brain chemistry. Of course it's that … but it's also a lot more than that.

I have a hard time defining religious experience (or spiritual experience, if you prefer), but I can describe it. At its most basic level, it's that feeling you get when you come across something so big, so powerful, and so strange that all you can do is stare at it and say *wow* but deep down you know it's not all that strange—you're connected to it in some way. It's seeing the ocean for the first time. It's seeing a deer or a bear or an eagle in the wild. It's leaving the city and looking up at truly dark skies and seeing more stars than you thought existed. It's realizing the light from some of those stars has been traveling through space for millions of years and is just now reaching Earth. It's realizing the universe is so big and you're so small but you're still a part of it all, a part of a whole that is greater than any of us. It's the feeling that these connections mean something more than the fact that they happen and wondering what that something is.

We have or can have these experiences all the time. We don't appreciate them as religious experiences and sometimes don't even recognize them as anything at all because we're too busy to stop long enough to allow ourselves to go from seeing a sunset to experiencing a sunset, much less wonder about it. And if we allow ourselves to wonder too much, we might start wondering about the direction of our lives, goals, and priorities. We might start thinking that meaning and happiness don't come from bigger houses, more expensive cars, and the envy of our neighbors. And we can't have that, now can we? Our whole economy would collapse if everybody started valuing religious experiences over buying stuff!

Joking aside, it is in the recognition and acceptance of these ordinary religious and spiritual experiences where we train our perceptive abilities for deeper, more powerful, and more meaningful experiences … which of course is one of the reasons people tune it out. If you think comparing your less than a century on this earth with dinosaur tracks that are 110 million years old is scary, try having a primal forest god tap you on the shoulder and tell you there are things he wants you to do for him.

These deeper and more intense religious experiences are even harder to describe than the more ordinary ones, in large part because our society has no common understanding of them. We're taught that people who hear voices are crazy and that people who do what the voices tell them to do are dangerous…even though we celebrate the heroism of Joan of Arc and wonder about the prophecies of Nostradamus. We tell ourselves that it was a long time ago when things were different and people weren't as educated as we are. We tell ourselves something, anything to distance ourselves from the unpredictability of an encounter with a god or other mighty spirit.

It is rare to hear audible voices or to see extraordinary things with your physical eyes. More frequently it's a voice in your head that isn't your usual self-talk voice, especially if it tells you something you didn't know or didn't really want to hear. It's seeing something ordinary and being left with the unshakable understanding that it means something more. It's a dream that's more than the routine sorting and filing of the day's events. It's divination that tells you something you know is important even though you wish it wasn't. It's a reading where the diviner repeats exactly what you heard and saw in a waking vision even though they had no way of knowing you had it.

Major or minor, ordinary or extraordinary, religious experiences are real. I get so annoyed when social scientists ignore religious experiences in their theories of the origins and meaning of religion. It's like trying to explain the popularity of basketball using only socio-economic theories, having never set foot on a court and experiencing the feeling of hitting a 15-foot jump shot and hearing the *swish* of the net.

Some people consciously choose to not interpret their experiences. "I saw the sun set, it was beautiful, and I was happy." This kind of approach doesn't set any expectations for future experiences that may not happen or that may not be as beautiful or make you as happy. Nobody can tell you you're wrong, and it doesn't carry any obligations to change the way you live. You had the experience, you noticed it, you'll remember it, and life goes on. It's a perfectly legitimate approach. Some people choose to demystify their experiences. "The sun appeared to set because of the rotation of the earth, and the interaction of the light with the atmospheric conditions at the time created colors that evoked tranquility and caused my brain to produce pleasurable chemicals." Now, there's a place for science, and I like knowing the facts. But our world is too dreary as it is, and if a beautiful sunset will help re-enchant it, I prefer to embrace the magic.

Other people choose to interpret their experiences religiously. They see how their experiences align with their ideas about the nature of the world and the way the universe works, and they decide (often intuitively) what their experiences mean and what they should do because of them. "The setting sun reminds me that my life is finite, but as a restful night leads to a new morning, so will my death lead to a new life, even though I can't know if that life will be physical, spiritual, or something I can't even imagine right now."

Of course, not all religious experiences are as pleasant as a sunset. Many of us have received messages with a theme of something like, "There's a storm coming—gather your tribe." We've been told to make offerings and go on pilgrimages. Some have been told to build temples, orders, and priesthoods. And a lot of us have been told to get ready, even though we aren't quite sure what we're getting ready for.

There's a lot of ground to cover between opening yourself to the wonder and awe of the full moon and doing something that can get you literally or figuratively burned at the stake. It's a journey. I wish I could tell you that you can turn back at any time, but it would be a lie. Religious experiences are meaningful—they bring a sense of purpose and they cause you to adjust your priorities toward values and virtues our mainstream world thinks are unimportant. Adjusting your priorities opens you to further experiences that bring more meaning to your life and reinforce your ideas that these values and virtues are more valuable than chasing what the talking heads on TV tell you to buy. Eventually you realize you can't go back to the way you were before because you see the world differently ... and you also don't want to go back to the way *you* were before.

Go outside this evening and watch the sun set. Find the moon in the sky and watch it grow brighter as the sun's light fades. See the stars as they start to twinkle and shine. If it's overcast, just watch as the sky slowly moves from light to dark. You're an educated person—you know the science of what you're seeing. Tonight, though, just let the sky speak to you. It may say nothing. It may say nothing for a month or two or ten, and then suddenly overwhelm you when you don't expect anything at all. That's the thing about religious experiences: they come in their own time and not according to our preferences and schedules. And that sky may say something that will change your life forever.

RELIGION AS RELATIONSHIPS

The English "religion" comes from the Latin *religare*, meaning "to bind together." Many things bind us together. This isn't about restricting or limiting or constraining people, and it's certainly not about controlling them. Rather it's about forming and maintaining respectful, reciprocal relationships.

The first relationship is with nature. When I was growing up, there were three kinds of religion. There was the fundamentalist Christianity preached at the small Baptist church my parents took me to. There was all other religion, which was judged by how close or how far (mainly how far) it was from that form of Christianity. And there was the intuitive spirituality I experienced when I went walking in the woods. At the time, I didn't have the context to understand that a very different form of religion was possible—I just knew the woods were a magical place where anything could happen and there was always something new just over the next hill. The woods were a safe place. Of course, there were rocks and thorns and occasionally deep water, and spiders and snakes—a few of which were venomous —but those could be managed with a little caution. Despite its risks (or perhaps because of them) the woods were a retreat from the demands of home, school, and church.

I'm under no illusions about the harsh realities of nature. Science, for its part, teaches literally what Paganism expresses poetically: we grew out of nature and are a part of nature. My religion seeks to acknowledge that relationship in ritual and in ordinary actions: walking outdoors, saluting the sun and the moon each day, sky-gazing and tree-hugging, and picking up trash on the side of the road in addition to other this-world actions that treat nature like the great mother she is.

The second relationship is with the gods. For all my years of study and devotion, I've never come to a conclusive answer as to what the gods are. Part of that is because the question is impossible to answer with any certainty, and part is because the best discourse on the nature of the gods is done at an intellectual level far above my typical conversational writing style. I'm a Druid and a priest, not a theologian. But I am sure of two things: there are gods, and I and many others have experienced their presence and their activity.

Some religions teach that their god is so far beyond humanity that the only proper response is unquestioning submission (and if you think I'm only talking about Islam, you're wrong). But while the gods are *more* than humans (older, stronger, wiser, to name a few qualities) and therefore are worthy of our honor and worship, they are not so far above us that we cannot enter into mutually beneficial and respectful relationships with them. We can; I do.

My relationships with the gods or rather with the handful of gods who have made themselves known to me are founded on meditation (listening for and to them) and prayer (speaking to them). They're founded on reciprocity, on making offerings to them and on giving thanks for what they give me. They're founded on mutual interests—telling their stories, respecting and preserving the natural world, and working for the sovereignty of all, just to name a few.

Some magicians and occultists treat the gods as though they're soulless forces to be invoked and manipulated as the magicians see fit. In fairness, this is not impiety so much as it's a radically different notion of who and what the gods actually are. If the gods are offended, they can let the magicians know themselves. I don't know about you, but I'm not looking for people in my life to order around. I want friends and teachers who speak their minds and don't simply repeat what I want to hear. I want co-religionists who will challenge me to learn and grow. I want people who will remind me of what I promised to do, and in doing so help me accomplish it. I want honest relationships, not business transactions. It's the same with the gods. My religion is built on relationships with them.

The third is our relationships with each other. Humans are not solitary creatures. Like other primates, we live in communities. Our capacity for language has enabled us to communicate and cooperate at levels impossible for other species, a factor that has led to us dominating the planet. Whether that's a good or bad thing or a little of both is another question.

We form families based on relationships of blood and relationships of caring. We form neighborhoods based on relationships of place. We form businesses based on relationships of needs and the ability to fill them. And we form religions based on relationships of common beliefs, practices, values, and our ideas about the way the world works and how best to interact with it.

My religious relationships begin locally, with my UU church and CUUPS group. We don't all believe the same things, even among the polytheists in our group. That said, our differences don't stop us from coming together to honor the gods, to promote their virtues and values, and to make the world a better place. I'm not a Heathen and am actively avoiding a couple of Norse deities (I tell them I've already got a full dance card), but I will happily take a part in a Gleichentag ritual to celebrate the Autumn Equinox and support my Heathen friends.

My religious relationships include people living far away who share my love of nature and the gods, especially my fellow Druids. They include Pagans and polytheists whose work I respect and whose counsel I value. We don't all know each other well, and we might very well run into serious conflicts if we tried to form an organization. However, we have common interests and can support each other, and so we do.

Shared meals have been a way to maintain relationships for a very long time. Imagine, if you will, a holy day long ago in ancient Greece. There will be purification. There will be a musical procession to an altar where a sacrificial fire is burning. Barley will be thrown. An animal, likely a bull, will be ritually killed. Some parts are offered to the gods, some parts are retained by the priests, and most of the meat is cooked and eaten by the members of the community. (This is an extremely high-level summary of one particular form of Greek sacrifice. For more details, read *Homo Necans* by Walter Burkert.)

There was a certain utilitarian quality to these sacrifices. Even a large family couldn't eat a whole bull; sharing it amongst the community just made sense. In coming together for a communal meal, the identity and unity of the group was reinforced—relationships were strengthened. By offering to the gods—that is, including them in the ritual and meal—

the relationship between the community and the divine was strengthened as well.

As anyone who has ever been in any kind of a romantic partnership will attest, relationships require work. Fail to do that work—provide for material needs, care for each other "in sickness and in health," talk and listen to each other on a regular basis—and the relationship will crumble. The same is true of our religious relationships. I value nature, so I spend time in nature. I value the gods, so I pray and meditate and make offerings and do their work in this world. I value my co-religionists, so I talk with them and gather with them to honor our shared traditions and celebrate together.

We have relationships with many persons: humans both living and dead; gods and spirits; and with other species and ecosystems. Will our relationships with them be respectful and for our mutual benefit, or will they be exploitative? Good relationships are based on hospitality and the interaction between hosts and guests. They're also based on reciprocity: I give so that you may give, so that I may give again.

Let us honor and strengthen our relationships.

ANCESTORS

My polytheism rests on a foundation of mighty ancestors.

If you're looking for the foundations of most polytheist religions, you don't have to dig very far before you run into ancestors. Ancestor veneration doesn't require special revelation; it comes intuitively even to committed atheists and monotheists. Go into their homes and you'll see pictures of grandparents on the wall, collections of mementos that could properly be called a shrine, and perhaps even family trees and histories.

Who are our ancestors? Some we knew in this life, some we know only their names and dates of birth and death, and some we don't know at all. But no matter how close or distant we are from our ancestors, they answer the question, "Where do we come from?" We look at old pictures and we see some of the same features we see in the mirror. We share a name or hear a tale and realize that could have been us. We do a bit of genealogical research and find roots in a faraway land…and sometimes living relatives too. All that reminds us that we're not alone in this world.

That's enough information that the impossible answers to where we ultimately came from are less troubling. If you know you came from your parents and grandparents, and they came from their parents and grandparents, and a long time ago some of them came from Ireland or Germany or Nigeria and who knows how long they had been there, that's enough ancestors to keep you busy remembering and honoring. If you're grounded in the recent past, the blurriness of the distant past becomes less and less troubling.

It is good and right that we honor our ancestors. It's only because of them that we're even here, much less that we have things like religion, culture, art, and the infrastructure that supports our lives. We can't pay them back, but we can thank them, remember them, and strive to be good ancestors for those who come after us.

Our ancestors' gifts continue long after they leave this world. We know that whatever hard times we're going through, we have an ancestor who went through something just as bad or worse. We know they got through it or we quite literally wouldn't be here. They faced famine and disease, invasion and war, plagues and floods. They moved—the story of humanity is the story of migration. I'm sure some of that migration was out of curiosity and adventure, but I'm just as sure more of it was due to dwindling food supplies or a lack of safety. They did what they had to do, and so can we.

Our ancestors are our spiritual allies. It's great to work with gods and with local spirits, but their goals and our goals don't always align. Our ancestors are spiritual beings who have a personal interest in seeing that we survive and succeed. They're usually accessible and willing to help when other spirits may not be.

Our experiences of our ancestors point toward an Otherworld. If someone you knew well has died, you've almost certainly dreamed of them. Is this simply your subconscious remixing your memories? Sometimes. But dreams remind us that our relationship hasn't ended, it's just changed forms.

And then there are those experiences of ancestors that are more than dreams, that are so real we can't ignore them. They do not "prove" the existence of life after death (much less what form that afterlife takes) but they point us in that direction.

Our contemporary families are more complicated than strict bloodlines. We have adopted families, blended families, and chosen families. Sometimes we use different vocabulary, but it's always been this way, with marriages, fosterage, and associations so tight they were called brotherhoods and sisterhoods. Those who came before us in these relationships are our ancestors too, and they are as deserving of our honor as our ancestors of blood.

Ancestor veneration and even ancestor worship is not polytheism—our ancestors are not gods (for the most part—a few ancestors do become gods). Likewise, polytheism does not require ancestor veneration … though few if any forms of polytheism ignore it. Ancestors and gods are both spiritual beings, however, and the multiplicity of ancestors points toward the multiplicity of the gods. Our intuitive impulse to honor our ancestors points toward the need to honor the gods. Our recognition of the gifts of our ancestors helps us recognize the gifts of the gods.

THE OTHERWORLD

Many of the world's cultures have some concept of an afterlife. Christianity teaches of a bifurcated afterlife (heaven or hell) completely removed from this life. The Egyptians promised a place with Ra in the Boat of a Million Years for those whose hearts are as light as a feather, but oblivion for everyone else. The Greeks (or at least, some of them) offered the Elysian Fields for heroes, a rather dull afterlife for the masses, and torment in Tartarus for those who particularly offended the gods. Celtic lore describes an Otherworld that is very similar to our world and that exists alongside it. Many times, visitors didn't even realize they were in the Otherworld until they saw something or someone that doesn't belong in our world. The Welsh *Mabinogi* describes how Pwyll was hunting and got separated from his party. He didn't begin to suspect he had wandered out of his own world until he encountered a pack of strange hounds with red markings, and he wasn't sure until he met Arawn, King of Annwn.

My own concept of the Otherworld is much like this. It is the land of the gods and ancestors, but it is not so very different from our own.

As with the story of Pwyll and Arawn, much of what we know about the Otherworld comes from the stories of our ancestors. Now, we live in a society where a substantial number of people read the Bible as though it was a history book. Pagans, of all people, should not fall into that fallacy. But that doesn't mean we should go 180 degrees in the other direction and assume these stories are complete works of fiction. Rather, they are myths that tell the stories of the Otherworldly experiences of our ancestors. We can have our own experiences of the Otherworld. On rare occasion we may get a glimpse into the Otherworld with our physical eyes, but usually we experience the Otherworld through dreams and journeying, including journeying in ritual.

Our ancestors were not so very different from us, so it is likely that their stories have similar origins to our own stories. They're reports of what someone in ancient Ireland or Britain or Gaul saw, heard, felt, and did. Have the stories been dramatized? Almost certainly. Have they been enhanced? Probably. Is there wisdom in them anyway? Absolutely.

They are myths—stories that communicate timeless meaning and values. Don't fall into the trap of the biblical literalists, who insist that all stories are either perfect transcripts of exactly what happened or they're meaningless. Religion is not just mythology, *but* mythology is an important part of religion.

The Celtic Otherworld is not a land of peace and perfection. Arawn needed Pwyll's help to defeat a rival king. Pwyll did so with one blow of his sword, then refused to perform the coup de grâce and end his opponent's suffering. The Otherworld is much like our own, only more.

Are the various Otherworlds, Underworlds, and Afterlives different cultures' impressions of one wider reality? Are they different sections of one great Otherworld? Or are there multiple Otherworlds for multiple cultures and religions? I don't know. In this world we are all different people in different lands but share the same planet. I suspect the Otherworld is similar. Let's not pretend we know more than we do … but let's also not dismiss what we do know, especially what we can know from our own first-hand experiences.

When we look into the Otherworld we see strange things. Not perfect things, but things that are *more* than they are here. We see our ancestors, not wasted on their deathbeds as we last saw them but whole and healthy. We see heroes, filled not with perfection but with honor and valor. We see gods, the mightiest of beings, who are filled with virtue. We see mystery and magic. We see relationships that do not die, cauldrons that are never empty, and warriors who are committed to justice. We see things as they could be here.

Pagans—and I include myself here—often visualize the Otherworld as rural and pre-industrial. That's understandable, as it reflects what things looked like the last time our ancestral religions were widely practiced. It also reflects our desire for a simpler time … one that overlooks the benefits of modern sanitation and other technological advances. There is no harm in engaging in a little pleasant anachronistic dreaming. The harm comes when we assume the past was a Golden Age so great that the afterlife must surely look and feel exactly like it. This kind of thinking can cause us to devalue the present and undervalue the future. The Otherworld looks a lot like this world … our world here and now, for better and for worse.

Sometimes we're intrigued by the Otherworld because we have an Otherworldly experience. Sometimes it's because we're missing something here that we can find there. And other times there is something here we desperately want to get away from, even if we can't always put our finger on exactly what that is.

A mild experience of the Otherworld will change you in a mild way. You become intrigued, think about what happened and what it means, and wonder how you can repeat the experience. Your world is ever so slightly *more* than it was before. Of course, not everyone reacts positively to an Otherworldly experience. When challenged with something they've always been told isn't possible, some people double down on skepticism and materialism. They rationalize their experience away and insist that other peoples' experiences aren't real either. My religion is not a proselytizing religion—I have no need to convince them they're wrong. Instead, I'm convinced my experiences are real.

A major experience of the Otherworld will change you in a major way. What you've been told all your life doesn't matter anymore; what you've seen can't be unseen. You still don't know exactly what the Otherworld is or what its residents want with you, but you have no doubt it's all real … and that matters. You no longer fear death because you know it's just a portal into the next world. You're now immune to advertising or at least can see through it—a car is a way to get you where you need to go, not a statement of your worth as a person. Your priorities are changed.

Again, though, not everyone reacts positively. The implications of a real Otherworld, real gods, and real spirits can be scary, not just in a "this can't be possible" sense but also in the "what does this battle goddess want from me? What might she do if I fail?" sense as well. And sometimes, the fear is also something like, "If this is real then parts of the scary religion of my childhood might be real too." Parts of it are and parts of it aren't—you have to figure out which is which.

The Welsh idea that an encounter with the Otherworld will leave you "mad, dead, or a poet" isn't just pretty words. A massive first-hand experience of the Otherworld will send some people over the edge. As always, be careful what you wish for, and keep in mind that we still live most of our lives in this world. Obsession with the Otherworld can turn into escapism, and that's a shame because Paganism insists this world is good. Even with hurricanes and wildfires and humans who kill other humans, life is good and something to be enjoyed and savored, not transcended. The vast majority of people who have Otherworldly experiences manage just fine in the ordinary world, only now they bring an Otherworldly perspective to it and in doing so change the ordinary world and mainstream culture a tiny bit. This is how cultures are changed—one person at a time.

Some people are called to renounce this world and live in a permanent liminal state. These are the shamans and mystics, not bored suburbanites with a certificate from somebody's "shamanic institute." Shamans and mystics are people who died and came back and who regularly journey into the Otherworld for the benefit of their tribes, however "tribe" is defined. If such people are lucky, they'll have supportive family and friends who take care of their mundane needs. If not, they often struggle to navigate the ordinary world and sometimes end up medicated into submission … and both they and our world are worse for it.

This I know: I've seen the Otherworld. I've had firsthand experiences of gods and spirits that are more real than anything in this world. Those experiences changed the way I see this world and the way I live in this world. My life is better for these experiences, and not in a small way. So I write about my experiences, and I encourage others to explore their own Otherworldly experiences and to find the place for them in their religious and spiritual lives.

THE VEIL BETWEEN THE WORLDS

What keeps us from going back and forth between this world and the Otherworld on a daily basis? There is a boundary between them that keeps most of us from communicating with spiritual beings and all of us from doing it easily. It's what keeps the dead from returning to our world. In many modern Pagan traditions, that boundary is called the veil between the worlds. The veil is a metaphor, but the boundary— whatever it is—is real.

In Celtic traditions, it's not a veil but mists that separate the two worlds. I like that imagery better, and it more closely matches my first-hand experiences. While a veil—a curtain—has some thickness, it's essentially a two-dimensional object. Mists have both density and depth. Sometimes the morning fog is so thin you can barely tell it's there— other times it's so thick you can barely see taillights in front of you. Sometimes you drive though it into clear skies after a mile, other times it obscures a whole city. Likewise, sometimes the mists between the worlds are so thick we cannot see or hear our beloved dead. Other times they're so thin we can practically touch them. And when we wander into the mists—as some of us have been known to do—sometimes we get through quickly, while other times they're so dense we can't find the first landmark. Mists are a better description than a veil, but they're still a metaphor for an Otherworldly reality, the boundary between this world and the next.

Boundaries are an important feature of life, both spiritually and materially. If I drive east from Texas into Louisiana, all I see is a sign that says "Welcome to Louisiana." But if I drive north into Oklahoma,

I have to cross a real boundary: the Red River. One boundary is arbitrary, the other is tangible. We can argue that the difference between Texas and Oklahoma is also arbitrary, but there's no debate about whether the Red River is or isn't real, as you'll learn first-hand if you attempt to cross it without a bridge in place. The boundary between the ordinary world and the Otherworld is real, regardless of the metaphor used to describe it.

Modern Pagan tradition says that the veil between the worlds is thinnest at Samhain and Beltane, at the liminal times when summer changes to winter and vice versa. At these times, we can most easily communicate with the dead, and various spiritual beings can more easily cross over into our world. But now many Pagans are seeing this kind of crossover year-round. I've seen more and more reports of ghosts, spirits, and demons; accidents have been reported with no good explanation; reports of missing items turning up in impossible places are becoming too numerous to count. These things happen all the time, but they appear to be happening more and more frequently since about 2011 and especially since 2015.

I've seen some people speculate that malevolent magicians are working spells to shred the veil and allow more spirits to cross over into our world. That sounds too much like opening the hellmouth on *Buffy the Vampire Slayer* to me. Very few people who would do malevolent magic have the focus and discipline to develop the kind of skills it takes to be truly dangerous... not that they can't make a nuisance of themselves from time to time. Others suggest that there have been no changes to the Veil; what's changed is the number of people who are paying attention to the veil and Otherworldly happenings. It's entirely possible, and I suspect the greater interest is part of it.

I tend to think that like much in nature, the veil waxes and wanes in natural cycles, albeit very long ones. The stories of our ancestors tell us that the Otherworld used to be much closer to the ordinary world. If the Veil became thicker and more resilient at the same time as the dawn of civilization, perhaps it is now time for it to become thinner and softer again. If it's a natural cycle, it can't be reversed ... and what we're seeing is only the beginning.

At this point we're into full-blown speculation. I'm an engineer—I prefer hard evidence. But speculating about the Otherworld and the veil between worlds helps us build our model of the world and how it works. Some parts of our speculation are likely wrong but they do give us a place to start. The key is to hold our beliefs loosely and to be willing to change them when we have new experiences and come across new evidence. Let's do some speculating.

Let's begin with a look at time. Our Christian-influenced culture tells us time is linear. Time began at creation and will end on Judgment Day. A moment comes, passes, and is gone forever. Over the past three-hundred years or so, a corollary has evolved called the myth of progress. Things get better for each succeeding generation, an upward trend that will continue to the stars. Our socioeconomic system is based on a be-lief in perpetual growth, which a bit of casual examination will show to be in serious error.

Paganism sees time as cyclical. Things come and go and then come again. The Wheel of the Year turns, bringing us from the Summer Sol-stice to the Fall Equinox to the Winter Solstice to the Spring Equinox and then back to the Summer Solstice again. The moon waxes from dark to full, then wanes back to dark. Every January is similar to every other January, even though they're not identical. And Januaries are dif-ferent from Junes.

Not all cycles are perpetual. Empires rise. They may wax and wane for a while, but eventually they fall. Pharaonic Egypt lasted for over three thousand years, through what modern historians call the Old Kingdom, Middle Kingdom, New Kingdom, and the Ptolemaic Period. We can debate whether the Ptolemaics were really Egyptians (they were mostly Greeks trying to claim the heritage and authority of the pharaohs), but with the coming of the Romans the Egyptian empire was over for good. Rome itself would rise and later fall. Time, then, is not a linear progression of lesser to greater. Rather, it is a series of waxing and waning, of seasons and cycles.

Now let's look at some cycles in the natural world. The planets of our solar system revolve around the Sun over different periods of time. The Earth takes 365.25 days to go around the Sun. Mercury takes only 88 days, while Mars takes 687 days, Jupiter 11.9 years, Saturn 29.5 years (the astrological Saturn return), and Neptune 165 years. Pluto—for those who still consider it a planet—takes 248 years. These varying periods of revolution create the phenomenon of planetary alignment, although the planets never perfectly align. A 30° arc is about as closely aligned as they ever get. But individual planets and stars come into close alignment all the time.

This is not an astrological speculation. The point is that there are many seasons and cycles in our world, and when several of them align, unusual things can happen.

We're constantly aware of the Earth's seasons. Most of us know the last glacial period ended about twelve thousand years ago. What most of us don't realize is that there have been five major ice ages and some of them have lasted for hundreds of millions of years. We should be entering another period of glaciation about now, but we aren't—in part because of tiny variations in the Earth's rotation and orbit and due to our dumping so much carbon dioxide into the atmosphere. But sooner or later the cycle will resume and the current interglacial period will end.

Now that we've established a factual context of seasons, cycles, and alignments over time periods ranging from eighty-eight days (one year on Mercury) to 300 million years (the Huronian Glaciation), let's look at some of the shifts we're currently experiencing.

As we look for patterns and cycles, we move into the realm of theories that aren't fully developed, or at least not yet. The stories of our ancestors tell us the Otherworld used to be much closer to the ordinary world—they tell of wandering into the woods and finding yourself in Annwyn. Sail into the west and you may find yourself in the land of Manannán mac Lir. Zeus and Odin were known to walk bodily among mortals to test their hospitality. Something happened, and then the Otherworld got farther away or at least harder to reach. Some blame the expansion of civilization and its technologies. Some blame the rise of monotheism.

In truth, major shifts rarely have a single cause. Perhaps human-centered changes had something to do with it, but perhaps this world and the Otherworld naturally moved farther apart... and now they're moving closer together. We know the veil between the worlds naturally thins at Samhain and Beltane—perhaps it also thins and thickens on a scale that's thousands of years long.

The Western linear theory of time says that once the Otherworld faded, it was gone for good. But the Pagan cyclical theory of time says that if it faded, it will return at some point in the future. It appears that point in the future is now.

What I'm suggesting is going on is the "distance" (in quotes because I'm not talking about physical geography) between this world and the Otherworld is subject to cyclical variation, and we are entering a time when the two worlds are close together. The veil between the worlds thins and thickens seasonally and also on a longer time scale—possibly millennia long. We are in a time when the veil is extremely thin.

History tells us that in times of trouble, people turn to religion and magic even more than in other times. These are times of trouble, which means more people are working magic, which means more magic in the overall environment—a feedback loop that keeps getting stronger. Perhaps because of these changes or perhaps for their own reasons,

Otherworldly beings are returning to the ordinary world, creating another feedback loop and adding to the overall effect. All of these things (and possibly more) are coming together in something of a planetary alignment of changes in the spiritual and magical environment. It's not one thing or two things, it's all of them and the interactions between them.

Some factors of this change I can't even guess about. Is the alignment of factors just starting? Is it at its strongest? Or will the Otherworld grow even closer, the Veil even thinner, the magic even stronger, and the Otherworldly beings even more present in the ordinary world? How long is this going to last? A year? A hundred years? A million years? We can make some reasonable guesses as to when the last magical maximum periods ended, but we have no way of knowing when they started, so we can't even guess how long it will last.

It is good to understand the environment in which we work. The better we understand what's going on in the spiritual world, the better we can respond to it. This is one of the reasons so many of us practice divination. But while speculating about megashifts in the nature of reality is a helpful exercise, at the end of the day we still need to care for ourselves and our families, honor our gods and ancestors, and leave the world a better place than we found it … even if the world as we know it is crumbling around us. Let's think about this, but let's not obsess over it, and let's not let it keep us from doing what must be done.

That said, I'm going to keep wondering and speculating.

3

POLYTHEIST
FOUNDATIONS

IN MY FIRST BOOK, *The Path of Paganism,* I discussed the four centers of Paganism. This is a model of modern Pagan religion—four key concepts and practices around which Pagans gather. The four centers are nature, deities, the self, and community.

This book is deity-centered. When I was discussing titles with the editor, there was only one thing I insisted be included: polytheism. This book is about deeper explorations of modern Paganism but takes a distinctly polytheist approach. Polytheism isn't the only way to go deeply into Paganism, but it's the approach I've taken, so it's the approach I'm writing about.

As I mentioned in the introduction, I rely on the Anomalous Thracian's definition of polytheism: "the religious regard for many real gods." The gods are real, distinct, individuals with their own sovereignty and agency—the existence of the gods is not dependent on human thought and activity. Let's explore that definition in more depth.

Polytheism is focused on the gods. The gods are individuals. They are many. They are real. They have will and agency. They act in this world, sometimes through humans but sometimes on their own. They have great power and wisdom but are not omnipotent, omniscient, or omni-anything else. They sometimes take interest in humans and occasionally come to our aid, but that is not their primary role. They have their own desires, goals, and areas of responsibility, same as every other living being in the universe. In my polytheism, the gods are first. Not just because they're gods, but because they've shown themselves to be trustworthy and wise. Focusing on the gods and on their values and virtues allows me to be a part of something bigger than myself, something that will remain long after I'm gone.

Most polytheist religions include ancestors and spirits. I see gods, ancestors, and spirits as qualitatively similar (though not identical) beings. I honor the gods, so it makes sense to honor the ancestors and spirits as well. As with the gods, they are many, real, and individual. Ancestors of blood and spirit are likely to have an interest in the survival and success of their descendants, so they tend to be more accessible than deities. We often have common interests with the spirits, particularly the spirits of the places where we live.

Polytheist practice is grounded in hospitality and reciprocity. Hospitality is rooted in being a kind, polite, and generous host. If we invite spiritual beings to join our rituals, we want to make them feel like welcome guests, not start ordering them around and demanding they give us stuff. The world runs on reciprocity: I give, so that you may give, so that I may give again. A craftsperson does a service for you and you pay them. You do a favor for a friend and know that someday, they'll do something for you. Giving to the gods isn't appeasement or bribery. It's demonstrating that we understand the world runs on honest exchange.

I treat all living beings with respect. I treat the gods with reverence, for which the common definition is "a feeling of deep respect or awe." How can you not be in awe of mighty beings who, if not immortal (though I imagine they are), are at least centuries old, who have the perspective of the ages, and who continually demonstrate virtues? I do not debase myself—I too am a being of inherent value and worth. But whatever I am, the gods are more, and it is good and right to remember this.

I maintain my sovereignty even before the gods. I show the gods great deference because my experience has shown that going along with their requests and their plans is generally in my best interest, not because I fear what they'll do if I say no. Ultimately, I am responsible for my life—and if a god asks me for something I cannot or should not give them, then I must say no. That doesn't mean they can't take it anyway—they can. In my experience, however, they rarely do.

My polytheism is informed by my experiences of the gods. It is not an exercise in psychology or philosophy, nor is it historical re-enactment. It is a daily first-hand experience of their presence in prayer, meditation, and occasionally in direct ecstatic communion. I don't write much about my experiences of ecstatic communion because I can't. Not because it's forbidden, but because I can't adequately describe the experience of a deity merging their consciousness with mine, to some small extent. I'm an engineer trained in science, and I'm highly skeptical by nature. But in those moments, I have absolutely zero doubt that the gods are real and present.

My polytheism is open and subject to constant revision. Though I speak with confidence about what I've experienced and what I believe and think, I know that in matters of theology there is no such thing as certainty. No matter how strong my experience or how solid my scholarship, there's a chance I'm wrong. While I refuse to be agnostic, my integrity demands that I remain open to new information, ideas, and experiences. I'm in my third decade on this path; at this point I'm mostly making refinements, not wholesale changes to my worldview and belief system. But the day I stop learning will be the day I die.

My polytheism is a public polytheism. While my most intimate experiences of the gods must remain private, I am called by the gods I serve to be a public presence of polytheism. The loudest voices in our mainstream society insist there is only one god. The second loudest voices insist there are none. Ordinary people need to see that yes, some people do worship many gods. I do not proselytize, but I do have an obligation to publicize polytheism and polytheist religions.

My polytheism is practiced in community. I do not worship the gods only to enjoy the experience of their presence. I want to participate in their work, and in doing so, build a better world here and now. This requires working with other like-minded people. Sometimes this is other polytheists. We worship together, compare our experiences, discuss the results of academic research and how we can incorporate it into our polytheisms. We write books, teach classes, sing hymns, and build temples. We do other things too, but mainly we work together to become better polytheists and to build a stronger polytheist community. Sometimes this is other Pagans. We may not all see the gods in the same way, but we can come together for events like Pantheacon, Pagan Pride Day, and to help people who wander into the Big Tent of Paganism to find where they belong. Sometimes this is other open-minded folks of any religion or no religion at all. We work together for religious freedom, to care for nature, and to build a more just and compassionate world for all.

I cannot worship authentically alongside some people. If I attend a Christian worship service, I cannot recite a creed that claims there is only one god, and they cannot pour offerings to a god other than their own. But that's no reason Pagans and Christians can't work together to make our shared world a better place.

My ethics and my politics flow from my polytheism but are subordinate to it. I am a priest of two gods of nature, so caring for the natural world is a religious obligation for me. I have a sworn, non-priestly relationship with a goddess of sovereignty, so respecting every person, species, and ecosystem is a religious obligation for me. I have other relationships with other deities ; embodying their virtues and supporting their values is a religious obligation for me. Living in a quasi-democratic society, fulfilling these obligations requires me to participate in the political process, but that participation does not demand one specific political approach, particularly if my understanding of history and of human nature tells me an approach is unlikely to be effective and may have disastrous side effects.

Further, my polytheism requires that I work and worship with those who share my commitment to the gods and their virtues and values, even if their political approach is vastly different from mine. There is no place for racism, misogyny, homophobia, transphobia, or any other form of prejudice or hatred in my polytheism. It follows that if we agree on the goals but disagree on the means to achieve them, I cannot and will not exclude them from my community.

My polytheism doesn't require bashing anyone else's religion. I'm a polytheist, which means I think both monotheists and atheists are wrong. That said, I have no need to go into monotheist or atheist spaces (or into their conversations in the public square) and tell them how wrong they are. The principles of hospitality and reciprocity demand I not do so.

My polytheism requires the maintenance of healthy boundaries. The boundaries of my polytheism are low and flexible, but there is a point beyond which they must be enforced. If a monotheist or an atheist comes into polytheist space and starts telling everyone how wrong we are, I have an obligation to rebut them. If they persist, particularly if they make arguments that may be confusing to seekers and beginners, I have an obligation to show them the door.

Differing opinions within polytheism are welcome and fighting over ownership of terms is unhelpful, but differences demand clarity.

Inclusiveness is a worthy goal, but not if it means whitewashing significant differences in foundational beliefs and devotional practices. What I think is a significant difference may strike someone else as trivial, and vice versa. But our unity must be an open and honest unity. If we find we cannot worship together, we can and must still work together as part of the wider community.

This is my polytheism. This is the foundation from which I practice and from which I write and speak.

GODS, PANTHEONS, AND CULTURES

One of the hindrances to my early Pagan practice was the approach some 101-level books took with the gods: "Just pick a pantheon," with the assumption that the reader would pick one of three sets of deities: Celtic, Greek, or Norse. You were then supposed to figure out who was the patron of this function or that and invoke as needed.

I would not have called myself a polytheist at that time, but it still didn't seem right to me. I intuitively picked up on some of the problems with it, problems I wouldn't be able to fully articulate for several more years. This pick-and-choose approach was far from the only problem I had in my early Pagan years but it didn't work for me, and I couldn't move forward in my Pagan practice until I got past it.

The first problem was the idea of gods as functions rather than as persons. At one point I had a very specific need, so I prayed to a very specific Greek goddess and asked for her help. And I clearly heard back, "Who are you?" in about the same tone you'd use if someone you'd never heard of called you on the phone and asked for money. I explained who I was and what I wanted. In reply, I heard, "And just why should I help you?" I had enough sense to not reply, "Isn't that your job?" and instead made some vague promises of offerings and praise. I heard nothing ... and I got nothing.

The gods are not vending machines. Reciprocity is a prime Pagan virtue, but "I give so that you may give" is a long way from "Here's a sip of wine, now please give me stuff."

When we see the gods as persons and not merely as the personification of this or that natural force or ideal (which they may also be), then we can begin to know them as deep and complex beings with their own likes and dislikes, goals and desires. And when we know them as persons, we are far more likely to respect them as the holy powers they are.

The second problem was the idea of a pantheon as a complete, self-contained unit. Even among the Greeks' twelve Olympians, there were variations from time to time and from place to place. Zeus, Hera, Poseidon, and some others were constants; Hephaestus, Hermes, Hestia, and Dionysus were on some lists but not others. And that's before we get to the idea of the multiplicity of the gods. Zeus Olympios was understood and worshipped differently from Zeus Chthonios and Zeus Aetnaeus. If you simply pray to Zeus, which one is going to answer?

The idea of a Celtic pantheon is almost laughable. Are you talking about Ireland, Britain, or Gaul...or perhaps some of the older continental deities? What about Cernunnos and Danu, who have no mythology? It gets even worse when you try to pigeonhole them into functions based on a Victorian-era analysis of ancient Greece.

Pantheons are often presented like a corporate organizational chart based on function and hierarchy. It's better to understand them as a family tree: a collection of individuals who are related but who ultimately do their own thing.

The third problem was the idea that you can simply pick someone at random and go to work. Now, you don't have to wait to be tapped on the shoulder. Pursuing the gods (or rather, pursuing one or two or three specific deities) is a good and honorable thing. I was called by Cernunnos but pursued the Morrígan.

But like our human relationships, our relationships with deities take time to develop. Boundaries have to be negotiated and trust has to be developed. What do they want from you, and what are you willing to give? How long of a commitment are you willing to make? My commitment with the Morrígan took several years for me to work through. In contrast, when I first started studying Druidry, I thought Lugh should be my patron. That didn't work out like I expected, although a relationship did finally develop after many years.

"Just pick a pantheon" didn't work for me. The gods are persons, not functions. The many pantheons are complicated families, not corporate organizational charts. Relationships take time and effort to build and maintain.

THE AUTHORITY OF THE GODS

I'm not big on obedience, a trait I'd blame on the fundamentalist religion of my childhood but honestly, it's just me. I don't like to take orders from anyone. On the other hand, the older I get, the more I realize just how much I don't know—and the more I realize I don't have enough years left to learn everything I need to learn. If someone else shows they know more than I do, I'm going to listen carefully to what they have to say. If they show time after time that following their lead brings favorable outcomes, I'm going to listen very carefully.

This has been my experience with the gods, or at least, with the gods with whom I have an on-going relationship. This is why I respect the authority of the gods.

The authority of the gods is in their virtues. Some say the gods are the personification of the virtues and the natural forces they control. I see them as whole beings who are far more complex than that … though perhaps that just means virtues are more complex than we usually think. The authority of the Dagda is in his abundance and generosity. The authority of Brighid is in her inspiration and transformation. The authority of Isis is in her healing, nurturing, and magic. We can hold a philosophical debate as to whether these virtues are inherently good or if they are good because they help us live better lives, but they are unquestionably good. Accepting the authority of these virtues is a good thing. It follows that accepting the authority of the gods who embody them is also a good thing.

The authority of the gods is in their experience. Did the gods begin when they were first worshipped by humans? Did they begin as the Earth began? Have they always existed? No one knows. Leaving aside the matter of apotheosis and of new gods, it's fair to say that the gods are at least thousands of years old. How much have they seen? How much have they done? How much have they learned?

The pace of change in the contemporary world devalues elders—accumulated knowledge is outweighed by familiarity with new technology. But for all our marvelous magical toys, we are the same creatures who first developed the capacity for language over 100,000 years ago. Nature is in constant change, but it follows the same processes it's always followed. Observing and participating in these processes for more human lifetimes than we can comprehend gives the gods a perspective we can never have. The perspective of millennia carries an authority worthy of our respect.

The authority of the gods is in their vision. One of the most popular Pagan skills is divination—not the ability to "tell the future" (the future is not fixed) but the ability to see where you're going so you can make necessary course corrections. Sometimes this vision comes from observing trends and patterns in an intuitive but logical manner. Other times it comes from communication with spiritual beings whose insight is far greater than our own. Imagine insight based on what a god can see that is informed by pure virtues, calculated with the power of a god, and evaluated with the wisdom of a god. That's something I'll trust and something I'll follow.

Of course, we aren't always shown their full visions. In my own practice, I'm rarely shown than one step at a time … transparency is not one of their virtues. But I've worked with Cernunnos and Danu and others for years. When they've asked (or occasionally, demanded) that I do something, it's worked out well. Not always pleasantly and never easily, but it's been an honorable and necessary process that has helped me to learn and grow and contribute to the greater good. So when a god asks me to participate in something larger than myself with my one brief human lifetime, I respect the authority of their vision.

I respect the authority of the gods. My life has been better by deferring to the authority of the gods. But I am still responsible for my life and how I choose to live it.

The gods have their own agency—they live their own lives their own ways for their own reasons. Those reasons do not always line up with our own. A plain reading of the stories of our ancestors reminds us that the gods do not always have our best interests at heart. The experiences of contemporary polytheists remind us that our safety and comfort are not very high on their list of priorities. Do your interests line up with their interests? Are you willing to make the sacrifices—personal as well as ritual—they demand? If you can't answer yes to those questions, you may be better off rejecting the authority of the gods and going it alone.

Further, the gods I follow have shown little interest in micromanaging the workings of human society. Many things that are of great importance to us (rightly or wrongly) are of little importance to them. If the gods are silent, perhaps you're asking them to choose between vanilla or chocolate for you. Or perhaps they see you're trying to avoid taking responsibility for your own life and they decline to be enablers.

But where the gods choose to exercise their authority, I always respect it, and I usually defer to it. Their virtue, experience, wisdom, and vision are far greater than my own. When they speak, I listen.

HEALTHY BOUNDARIES AND
THE LIMITS OF INCLUSION

Centuries of monotheistic domination have left Paganism, polytheism, and other religions with some decidedly unhelpful assumptions about the way religion works in a free society. These assumptions show up whenever someone starts talking about the boundaries around their religion. It doesn't take long before someone else chimes in with the passive-aggressive comment, "Well, there's no room for *me* in your religion."

What makes you think there's supposed to be room for you in every religion?

Of all the world's many religions, only the conservative versions of Christianity and Islam claim to have exclusive possession of The Truth. Some others have an outward focus (Buddhism has a particularly strong missionary tradition), but they merely offer their ways to others. Only the conservative monotheists—more specifically to us, conservative Christians—insist that everyone must adopt their religion or suffer eternal damnation.

Centuries of Christian domination have left us with the idea that any "real" religion is intended for everyone. But as anyone who's ever spent time in a conservative Christian church knows, they'll take you "just as I am"…but you'd better change right away. You're expected to change your beliefs, your language, your sexual practices, and even how you spend your money. We remember they want everyone and forget they want everyone to be just like them.

In the hyper-individualistic twenty-first century, though, everyone expects a church to cater to them. And many churches do. Catholics, mainline Protestants, and Evangelicals can no longer count on each generation to take their parents' places in the same churches, and they haven't for fifty years. They're struggling to "remain relevant" and they're desperate to attract members no matter what it takes. My Facebook feed includes some Christians searching for "what meets my needs" and other Christians complaining about entertainment replacing worship. Given these two cultural forces, it's no surprise many people in our wider society (from which Paganism and polytheism largely draw its members) don't know what to make of religions that 1) don't claim to be for everyone, and 2) don't attempt to cater to everyone.

The only way a religion can be for everyone is to insist everyone conform to their way of thinking and living. Daesh (the so-called Islamic state) claims their version of Islam is for everyone—I doubt anyone reading this wants to live under their rule. But if you go to the other extreme and try to include everyone's theologies and practices, you end up with something so watered down it's meaningless.

I regularly encourage beginners to dive into a new tradition wholeheartedly. Ask questions and walk away if you get ethically dubious answers, but otherwise do everything even if some of it doesn't make sense to you. When you're a beginner, you don't know what you don't know, particularly in mystery traditions where wisdom is revealed in stages. But if you pay attention and practice mindfully, sooner or later you start to develop your own religious identity. You believe the gods are this and not that. *This* ritual form is inspiring, and *that* form bores you silly. *This* social structure is helpful and *that* one is harmful. Nature has a certain importance, not more and not less. Your gods demand you take this action, forbid you to take that one, and all these others don't matter one way or another. All of a sudden you have boundaries and priorities. Some are rigid and others are flexible, some are critical and others are "nice to have," but they're all there.

And guess what? So does every religious group in existence, from the informal coven that meets in your neighbor's back yard to the UU church across town to international Druid orders to Tibetan Buddhism to the Roman Catholic Church. They all have boundaries and priorities ... and probably none of them match up exactly with yours.

So what are you to do when you go looking for a group to practice with and for a community to be a part of? You don't want to change your identity to satisfy them, and they aren't going to change their identity to satisfy you. Is there really no room for you in any religion? That can't be right, or we wouldn't have covens and orders and churches and such. You can't get 100 percent of what you want in a group or a tradition. But you can probably get 70 percent, or 80 or maybe even 98.

I'm a Pagan and a polytheist, but I'm also a Unitarian Universalist. What's a polytheist doing in a UU church, where an old joke says, "Unitarianism is the belief in one god, at most"? They're good people doing good work I support. They support environmental care, religious freedom and diversity, and full acceptance of everyone no matter their gender and orientation. And many of them are my friends. They don't affirm my polytheism but they do accept it, and they provide a home for Pagan-oriented UUs and UU-oriented Pagans. When I speak at Sunday services I usually talk on Pagan-oriented themes, but I do so in ways that are accessible to everyone. If I was only a UU I'd feel like something was missing, but I don't have to limit myself to one religious organization.

My Druidry is religious while most of OBOD is loosely spiritual. Why am I still in OBOD? They have the best distance learning program in the Pagan world … and possibly in the rest of the world as well. They teach spiritual techniques that are helpful in any religious tradition (at least, any open-minded tradition). They present Druidry to thousands of people all over the world, and many of them are my friends. OBOD by itself has never been "enough" for me—I was an active member of Denton CUUPS when I started the Bardic grade. But it has been and remains an important and fulfilling part of my spiritual life, and I'm happy to continue supporting it.

What about Ár nDraíocht Féin (ADF)? They're Druids, they're polytheists, and they have a strong public presence—surely I'm a 100 percent match with them, right? Nope, not even ADF. I have no arguments with

ADF's beliefs and structures, but their Core Order of Ritual—while extremely effective—isn't what I need when I need to lead a public ritual outside that structure. I'm also rather fond of some of the magical ritual elements that ADF rejects (because they're not part of indigenous Indo-European religions) but that OBOD includes.

There is room for me in all these organizations even though none are an exact match with my own beliefs and practices—that is, with my own religious identity. I don't have to change my identity to be a part of them, and they don't have to water down their identity to accommodate me. When I'm in one of their services or rituals I respect their boundaries and priorities and participate within them. When I hear UUs speak of "God" in monotheistic or even nontheistic language, I remember that in this context, the singular "God" is not what's most important. What's most important is a group of people coming together to form an open, caring, active religious community.

As with all things, there are limits: I can't be a Baptist even if they do good work on disaster relief. I can't be part of a religious tradition that believes their god is going to condemn the vast majority of people to eternal torment for believing the wrong thing. And someone who believes that can't be a Unitarian Universalist. I have my limits and so do you. But not every limit is a hard limit, and not every limit has equal priority. So no, there's not room for you in every religion, and your religion shouldn't try to make room for everyone. But there's probably room for you in any religion you care to be a part of so long as you don't expect to find a perfect match.

THE DEEPER CALL

4

I LIKE IT HERE—WHY DO I HAVE TO LEAVE?

To say I grew up in a stable home would be a massive understatement. My parents were married for almost fifty years. I lived in the same house until I left for college. I never changed schools except for promotions. I wanted to get away from home, but that was the ordinary teenage desire for independence. I never had wanderlust—I wanted to get away from home and build a new home the way I wanted it to be ... and then stay there.

As an adult I've made four cross-country moves. Two of them were to get away from a bad job, but the other two were because a good job went away and I had to move to find a new one. I like stability. If a situation is good, my preference is to stay there and use it as a foundation for further growth, not to walk away because something else might be better. It actually might be worse. But if I hadn't made those four cross-country moves—including the two I didn't want to make—my life would be so much less than it is now, in every way.

Few people are fortunate enough to grow up as Pagans. Most of us have an origin story wherein we find Paganism after a long search or stumble upon it out of sheer luck or the grace of the gods. Maybe we dive right in or maybe we take things in stages … or degrees, depending on your tradition. Eventually we find what works for us and we get comfortable with it. Our Paganism becomes stable. For some, it means recognizing the Divine in many forms, especially the Divine in Nature. For others it means celebrating the Wheel of the Year. It may mean setting up a shrine to our ancestors, or an altar to our patron deity. Or it may mean taking the vows of a priest and serving our gods and our community in a leadership capacity. There are many varieties of stability and none are intrinsically better than the others.

Some people find stability and are there for life. Others find stability but then in a year or two (or ten) they start hearing a call—from a new deity, to form a new group, or to explore the boundaries between this world and the Otherworld. Whatever form it may take, it is a call to leave stability behind and do something they've never done before. Perhaps it is something no one else is doing … or at least that you know of. Maybe there's a guidebook for the journey, but more likely they'll end up traveling off the edge of the map.

In the tarot, the 8 of Cups shows a cloaked figure walking away into dark mountains. Behind him are eight neatly stacked cups. He's leaving behind something of value, and given the cups' association with emotions, probably something that made him happy. The notes I took from my tarot teacher many years ago say, "Walking into the unknown. A new adventure. Breaking emotional attachments. Leaving the familiar to seek spiritual enlightenment. Leaving what is safe and known." It's time to move on.

In chapter 3 we covered how this world and the Otherworld are closer together than at any time in recent history. Why is that? How does it work? More importantly, what does it mean for our day to day lives? We don't know. How are we going to find out? By collecting experiences from many sources and doing some good data analysis. We'll find out by journeying and divination, and through communion with gods and spirits. Some of us are going to have to do some things our mainstream society says are impossible. We know they're very possible, but we also know risk is involved and we're no experts. Someone is going to have to do it and then write about how it goes.

Pagans are notoriously skeptical about institutions, but there are institutions we need now and more we will need as the movement grows. Someone is going to have to build them, and do so as Pagan institutions not Christian or secular institutions with a coat of Pagan paint. How do we do this? I don't know—someone is going to have to figure it out. Maybe that's someone else's job. Or maybe it's yours.

Your period of stability prepared you for this. Now, I hear some of you screaming, "What stability?!" Just because your life in total has been anything but stable doesn't mean your Paganism isn't. What is your Paganism about? What do you do? Have you been doing it for a while? Are there sacred stories you've heard so many times you know them by heart? Do you no longer require a reminder that Lughnasadh is coming and there's something you need to do to observe it? Do you make regular devotions to your gods and ancestors, even if "regular" isn't as often as you feel it should be? Do you have a familiarity with whatever it is you do? Then your Paganism is pretty stable.

Stability gives you a time when you can stop thinking about Paganism and just be a Pagan. It allows things you know in your brain to sink into your heart, your soul, your whole being. When you know what you need to know, you're ready to take a step forward. Maybe you're on a well-defined path and know where you're going. Maybe it's time to ask for your second-degree initiation. Maybe it's time to wrap up the OBOD Ovate gwersi and move on to the Druid grade.

Or maybe it's time to head out into open seas with nothing but the stars to guide you.

When my first good job went away, I could have said, "I don't want to leave my home town. I'll be happier if I stay here, even if I have to take a lesser job to do it." I could have done that, but I would have missed the experience of living in different parts of the country. And while I would not have regretted missing out on the job from hell that first move turned out to be, even that bad experience helped clarify that my true calling wasn't in business.

Maybe your Paganism feels right just like it is. Maybe you don't want to move on. Your life, your Paganism, your choice. For many people, staying in your stability is the right choice. But maybe what used to be stability now feels like a plateau. Maybe what used to be calm seas are now the doldrums. Or maybe you just know there's something more out there and you've got to see it for yourself.

Maybe it's time to go deeper.

LEARNING TO TRUST OUR OWN EXPERIENCES

The 1933 Marx Brothers film *Duck Soup* is the first recorded expression of a phrase that's funny but also deeply important: "Who ya gonna believe, me or your own eyes?" Decades later, comedian Richard Pryor used it when his wife caught him in bed with another woman: "Who you gonna believe, me or your lying eyes?"

Our mainstream culture tells us to ignore our own eyes and instead believe what the talking heads on television tell us must be true. In the political world, facts don't seem to matter. Some of this is a question of interpretation: liberals and conservatives have different ideas about what's important, a difference in moral instincts. Beyond that, we've seen plenty of studies that show when people are presented with evidence against what they believe, they discount it or flat-out deny it, and then double down on their established beliefs. Apparently, the human desire to feel like we've always been right is greater than our desire to actually be right. There has never been a greater need for clear, honest, independent thinking. There has never been a greater need to ignore what the mainstream culture tells you and to pay attention to what your senses—all your senses—tell you is happening.

Children believe in magic because they experience magic and they haven't yet been taught "better." They have far more and more powerful past life experiences than adults, possibly because they're still partially connected to where ever we were before we came into this world. They also play with other children regardless of color and appearance, because they haven't yet been taught that some people are "better" than others. But it isn't long before those with a vested interest in keeping things the way they've always been start laughing at their silly ideas, teaching them the way the world really works (a necessary thing, up to a point), and reprogramming them to become "productive members of society" (a very problematic thing). We're taught to distrust our own observations and especially our feelings, and to instead trust in consensus reality—the vague and unreflective opinions of the collective majority, as shaped by those with power and wealth.

We're told to grow up, to listen to the authorities, and to join the cool kids who are too sophisticated for "fantasies." Some of us are told our magical and spiritual experiences are "of the devil"—a deception designed to steal our immortal souls. Some of us are told both ... which in my case had the interesting effect of helping me decide that since both of them couldn't be right, they were both probably wrong and I'd be better off figuring it out on my own.

This has not been an easy path, but it's been a very rewarding one, and one I heartily recommend.

The best way to believe in magic is to do magic. Now, you have to put some work into learning what real magic is and isn't and what real spells are and aren't. If you think mindlessly repeating something you saw on TV is going to bring you anything, you're going to be disappointed. Invest a little time learning sigil magic or traditional witchcraft, however, and you'll start seeing results in a hurry. My first spells were straight out of Scott Cunningham's *Earth Power,* which is a long way from "serious" magic, but it worked well enough to convince me this was real beyond any doubt.

The best way to believe in the gods is to worship the gods. Read their stories. Sing their songs and read their poetry aloud. Meditate on their values and virtues. Make offerings to them. Then listen for their presence. Listen for that voice that seems like it's in your head except it's telling you things you didn't know ... and frequently, things you'd rather not hear even though your heart and your head tell you they're true. Be persistent, and be present in good times as well as bad—how would you respond if someone ignored you for years and then called you up out of the blue to bail them out of a bad situation? The gods are not so very different from ourselves.

Vision problems and optical illusions are easy to recognize; your eyes aren't lying. Neither are your ears, or your skin, or your innermost feelings.

But your ego will lie to you when it hears something that challenges what you've always believed. Your fears will lie to you when they see something that means you may have to change. Your insecurities will lie to you when they think you may have to step outside of what your friends and family and coworkers insist is real ... conveniently ignoring the fact that they're dealing with their own egos, fears, and insecurities at the same time.

Learning to trust your senses is an act of will. And like so many other parts of ourselves, the will is strengthened by exercise.

Being naïve and credulous is no virtue. Jumping to otherworldly conclusions is just as bad as jumping to materialist conclusions. Evaluating and interpreting religious and magical experiences requires discernment to put them into context, figure out what they mean, and decide how to respond. But honest and helpful discernment begins by trusting your senses, accepting that what you experienced actually happened, and refusing to rationalize it away out of fear or embarrassment.

Some religious and magical experiences are so strong they change your life on the spot, but most are subtle. When they are more subtle, they are easier to accept … and also easier to explain away. Don't. Examine the evidence, and if your best explanation is completely mundane, so be it. You're after the truth no matter where it leads you. And when the truth leads you to magic, accept it. Your senses may sometimes confuse you, but they will not lie to you. Consensus reality lies to you every single day. But don't take my word for it—go see for yourself.

WHY PAGANS DON'T TALK MUCH ABOUT DEPTH

Pagan and magical practices are still occasionally called "the occult" (meaning "hidden") even though it's been more than sixty years since Gerald Gardner went public with Wicca, and even though there has never been a time when magic was truly hidden from ordinary people. There is still a persistent idea that deep practices are dangerous and thus not safe for ordinary people. And some things are sacred—we do not want them profaned (i.e., made ordinary) by people who have no understanding or appreciation for their value.

I have mixed feelings on the secrecy surrounding Pagan practice. Yes, things that are esoteric (that is, of specialized or limited interest) are usually dangerous, but keeping our deepest practices and experiences hidden away is also dangerous. We live in a time when the deeper aspects of Paganism, polytheism, and magic are needed more than ever. Can we open these things up to a wider audience without turning them into crap? As someone who often rants against least common denominator Paganism, I recognize the risk.

I'm neither an occultist nor an intellectual; I'm a Druid and a priest who serves a local community in person and writes to serve a wider community, so part of my job is to make these deep practices accessible to anyone with a general interest and willingness to do the necessary work. In addition to making them available and accessible, it's also my job to make sure they remain authentic.

Most people aren't interested in depth. Let's be honest: only a small percentage of the followers of any religion are actually interested in ritual, devotion, theology, and mystical practices. If it seems like it used to be better in the Pagan world, that's because in the early days it was hard to be a Pagan. Listen to the stories some of our elders tell about how hard it was to find books on witchcraft, much less a coven willing to take them in. The only people who made it were those who were committed enough to keep looking until they found it.

There are some groups and traditions that maintain high barriers to entry. They have that right and I understand their logic. If your tradition demands teaching one-on-one, then you can only take a few students and will want to make sure you invest your time in those who are truly committed. But the religions of our ancestors weren't just for a few, they were for everyone. Only a few were priests or seers or shamans, but there was a place for ordinary people too.

I grew up listening to Baptist preachers screaming, "Why aren't all of you as committed as I am?" from the pulpit, and it's the last thing I want in my Paganism. Our Pagan and polytheist religions should not be all-or-nothing. My vision for the future of Paganism and polytheism is that there's a place for everyone at the level they wish to participate. I want everyone who will to hear the message that nature is sacred and deserving of our reverent care, that there are many gods who call us to worship them in many ways, and that the world is not dead and mechanistic but rather inspirited, enchanted, magical, and alive.

Some of us *are* called to depth, however. I'm thankful to live in a time and place where with a few clicks I can have English translations of ancient manuscripts delivered to my door. And if I had to hunt for books, I would. I might have been reluctant to look for a Pagan group fifty years ago, but I definitely would have asked around. Daily spiritual practice, group practice, ecstatic practice, and writing and talking about all of it are a big part of my life. I share much of that through my writing.

Deep Paganism, polytheism, and magic are very important to me and some of my friends. As Druids, priests, priestesses, elder witches, and other spiritual leaders, we can't force-feed anything to those who don't want it. Our public work has to be accessible to seekers, beginners, and those who just want to honor the gods and go about their daily lives.

But I have to keep doing the deeper work. It's such a part of my life now I'd feel empty without it. I'd also have a forest god and a battle raven kicking my butt up one side and down the other. I've made promises and promises must be kept.

I can't do all this work in public. Those who say it's dangerous are right. But I can do it alone, with a few others, and in small groups of like-minded folks, not all of whom are experts and elders—some are quite new but have shown deep respect for this work and the desire to do it. And that ability, desire, and willingness to do the work means everything.

We need to pull back the curtain from time to time. The Christian version of what you get when your primary goal is to avoid scaring or offending anyone is mainline Protestantism. With apologies to my mainline Protestant friends (many of whom are good people doing good work) there is little spiritual power in their churches. They've been in decline for fifty years and there's no end in sight.

Paganism is growing because it speaks to our need for a connection to nature, to the gods, and to our ancestors and their ways. It's growing because it's a participative religion—no sitting and listening to sermons. And it's growing because it's a religion of magic.

Every now and then, we need to pull the curtain back and remind everyone that we're not just dancing around the flowers (not that there's anything wrong with dancing around the flowers). There are gods and spirits; both can influence our lives. The Fair Folk are real and are not all cute and Disney-fied. Magic works, for good or for ill. You can't prove it and sometimes you can't see it with your physical eyes, but you can experience it and feel its effects. And sometimes those on the other side of the curtain decide to rip it open themselves.

Some people will see the real stuff and run screaming. So be it; it's not for everyone. Some will decide to stick to dancing the Maypole and reciting the Charge of the Goddess…but they'll know there's something more behind the curtain, if they ever need it. Some will decide they like what they see. They'll start asking questions and trying things out for themselves, and our deeper practice groups will have another member.

The line between religion and culture isn't nearly as strong as our Protestant-influenced society likes to think it is. The more people begin to celebrate nature, the gods, and magic the more they will move away from a culture built on exploitation, dominion, and materialism. Paganism is the future. The distant future to be sure (cultures don't turn on a dime) but the future nonetheless. Let's make sure it's a deep future, even if only a few of us are willing and able to explore its depths.

PART 2:

PRACTICE

5

DEVOTIONAL PRACTICE

DEVOTIONAL PRACTICE BEGINS WITH a choice: a deity to worship. Usually this is easier than it sounds. Most times when someone asks me about starting a devotional practice, a god is already in their life and encouraging them to begin. If there's more than one, you may be able to honor them together, or you may need to honor them separately, particularly if they are associated with different ethnic and cultural traditions. You might also choose to start with one and add others later. As always, I recommend you start small and don't overcommit. If there's no god in your life at all, then pick someone. Pick someone whose stories intrigue you, whose values match your own, or whose virtues would be helpful in your life. As with our human relationships, our relationships with the gods can be initiated by either party.

Create a shrine. A shrine is many things: a place for prayer and meditation, a place for offerings, a mystical center. A shrine isn't the same thing as an altar, the main difference being that a shrine is a mostly static place of honor while an altar is an active sacred space where work is done. Find a space you can dedicate to this purpose. I use a piece of finished plywood on top of a filing cabinet. Others use dresser tops, bookshelves, or cabinets (which can be closed to prevent questions from religiously troublesome visitors). A few have purpose-built furniture or outdoor shrines. While humans have a long and noble tradition of creating beautiful religious structures, don't let the desire for something perfect stop you from creating something useful right now.

What goes on or in the shrine? A representation of the gods and the items necessary to honor them. For me, that's statues, candles, and incense. Don't forget to leave working space for offerings. If you don't have a statue, can't afford or find one that strikes you as right, find another representation of the gods: a picture, a candle, a stone—pretty much anything that helps you connect to them.

Pray. Speak to the gods. Ancient prayers are good. So are contemporary prayers written by priests and devotees. So are your own words that express the yearnings of your heart. Calling them by names, titles, and epithets is good, if only because it reminds you of who you're talking to. Express your admiration and devotion. Give thanks where appropriate. Ask for what you want but consider who you're speaking to. Is your request something important or something trivial? And remember the principle of reciprocity: if you expect to receive, you should expect to give.

Be careful what you offer. If you say, "I'll do whatever you want me to do," they may take you up on it in ways you never considered. My experience has been that the gods are mostly (not always) lenient with beginners but much more strict with those of us who should know better. Pray respectfully and pray mindfully, but most importantly, pray.

Meditate. If prayer is speaking to the gods, meditation is listening for the gods. Many Pagans learn meditation from Buddhists; the practices they teach are indeed helpful. That said, emptying your mind is not the aim of polytheist meditation except to the extent that shutting down the monkey mind is helpful in hearing the often-faint voices of the gods. Listen, but do not expect to hear with your physical ears. Stay attentive for things to pop into your head you had no way of knowing. Look for coincidences stacking up. Pay attention to your dreams.

How do you separate the voices of the gods from your own inner self? It's hard to do at first; we aren't taught how to listen for the gods as children. Does something tell you what you want to hear? Does it tell you everything is OK just as it is? Does it play on your fears? Does it tell you things would be great if other people would just stop screwing things up? That's probably *you* doing the talking. But if it challenges you to embody the virtues of the gods, take on work you know needs to be done, or calls you to rethink your whole way of looking at the world, that's probably one or more deities.

Make offerings. The world runs on reciprocity: "I give so that you may give." This is true in our relationships with humans and it's just as true in our relationships with the gods. Do the gods really need our offerings? I don't know. I do know that offerings have been a part of devotion at least since the beginnings of organized religion, a tradition that continues to this day even in Christian churches both modern and traditional. More importantly, I know the gods have asked for offerings. Food and drink are the most common offerings, but sometimes other things are requested or required. Offerings can be formal or informal so long as they're offered reverently. And remember, a libation without a prayer is just a spilled drink.

Study. When a person is important to us, we want to learn all we can about them. That a whole industry exists around the lives of celebrities confirms this point and makes a sad statement about the priorities of our culture. If a god is important to you, learn all you can about them. Read their stories, talk to their priests about their experiences, read mainstream scholarship about the people who first worshipped them and how they lived. If you're able, visit sites sacred to them. This is easier for some than for others, but there is something out there for almost every deity known to humanity. Look for it, study it, and let it teach you more about them.

Do devotional reading. Study brings facts. Devotional reading brings experience and wisdom. Read a poem dedicated to your chosen deity. Sing a song to them. Read a story of someone's intimate experience of them. There are several devotional anthologies available (see Bibliography and References). There are more devotional blogs and websites than I can count. The approach and the quality of the writing varies widely, but with a bit of digging you can find something appropriate for you. Read about them and let what you read help you to hear them when they speak to you.

Review and refine. Start small: pick one or two of these practices. After you've done it diligently for a couple of weeks, add something else. At regular intervals (maybe every other week at first, then once a month, then once a quarter) review your practice. How's it going? What's working well? What's hard and needs more effort? What's just not working and needs to be dropped or changed? Make adjustments as necessary.

Mainly, listen. Devotion brings us into closer communion with the gods. As your practice grows and matures, they will usually let you know what needs to happen next. Sometimes it's something so simple you wonder why it's important. Do it anyway. Sometimes it's something so difficult you wonder how you can ever do it. Do it anyway. Sometimes you don't hear anything. Keep practicing anyway—divine relationships grow at their own pace.

There is no substitute for a consistent, reverent, devotional practice. May all your offerings be accepted, and may you grow deeper in your devotion to the gods.

THE PAGAN PRACTICE OF PRAYER

Many—perhaps most—Pagans have a broken relationship with prayer. We were forced to pray as kids. We suffered through long and boring prayers in church and before meals. Some people tell us prayer is the answer to everything, while others tell us prayer accomplishes nothing. And we all know people (Christian *and* Pagan) whose prayers resemble a four-year-old's Christmas list, which is enough to turn us off of the practice of prayer. And that's a shame, because prayer is one of the most basic and most helpful spiritual practices in virtually every religion.

For all the rules and mystery around prayer, it's a very simple thing: prayer is talking to the gods. Paganism is a religion (or religions, if you prefer) of relationships, and healthy relationships require constant communication. That's why meditation (specifically the kind of meditation that focuses on listening) is also important—we don't want to monopolize the conversation. The purpose of prayer is not to persuade the gods to give us stuff, nor is it to reinforce fragile egos with constant praise. Like conversations with friends and family, our conversations with the gods draw us closer to them. It reminds us to listen for their presence, and to keep their virtues and values foremost in our lives.

Some prayers are very formal and carefully scripted. They often follow a prescribed formula such as invocation —> praise —> request. Any ancient prayers you might come across are almost certainly scripted because unscripted prayers are rarely written down. If you're going to use a prayer over and over again or in a public ritual, it makes good sense to write it carefully. Make sure it says exactly what you want it to say. Make sure it flows and that it's grammatically correct. If it's not, make sure you're breaking grammar rules on purpose and not out of ignorance or carelessness. Make sure it doesn't mindlessly copy the language or format of the prayers of another religion. If you're speaking to your gods on behalf of a gathering, make your prayer as good as you can get it.

Other prayers are more conversational, wherein we speak to the gods as we might speak to someone standing bodily in front of us. Perhaps we have a great need and describe it in detail. Perhaps we want to negotiate the terms of an agreement to clearly delineate what we will do and what we won't. Or perhaps we want to express the yearnings of our hearts and simply speak. Of my four daily prayers, two are entirely scripted. The other two are partially scripted with places for conversational prayer. My ritual prayers are always scripted.

What do you say in prayer? Invocation is calling a god and asking them to hear your prayer. It is common to address a deity by multiple epithets. Part of this is to make it perfectly clear who you're talking to. But another part is so you remember who you're talking to.

Praise is recounting their virtues and their great deeds. Few if any of the many gods are insecure and need (or want) to be propped up by sycophants. But by praising the gods we are reminded of what is truly praiseworthy, and thus how we can best live our lives. If the gods have been generous to you, say thank you. If they granted your request, say thank you. If they declined to grant your request and you realize they did you a big favor because you asked for something you didn't really want, say thank you. There are many things we enjoy that we did not earn. The least we can do is express our gratitude.

Express your devotion. Which of their virtues do you most admire? Say it. What did they do for you that you really appreciate? Say it. How would you talk to your grandmother or to a favorite uncle? What would you say if a social or political leader you admire came to visit you? The gods are more than any of these things, and it is best to approach even familiar deities with reverence, but expressions of devotion and love are always appropriate.

The gods are persons, not vending machines into which you insert offerings so that blessings are dispensed. Even now I see some Pagans who have no qualms about approaching a deity they've never met and asking for huge favors. It's an approach that works about as well as a stranger walking up to you and asking for a substantial gift. That said, if you need something, ask for it. If you have a relationship with a deity, they're more likely to help you out of a difficult situation, particularly if you need something to be able to accomplish a task they've set in front of you. It is always good to ask for healing for yourself and your loved ones. Remember that the world runs on reciprocity. If a god grants your request, they may later ask you for something in return—that's how my relationship with the Morrígan began.

While we all want to avoid sounding like a kid sitting on Santa Claus's lap, there is nothing wrong with speaking the desires of your heart to the gods. What is it you want most? What is it you value most? What calls to you, perhaps softly and perhaps with a screaming voice? Say it. Tell the deities with whom you are acquainted how you feel. And then listen for their response.

I speak of "the gods" here, but as a polytheist I never pray to them collectively. I am a priest of Cernunnos and Danu, a Druid of the Morrígan, and a devotee of Brighid and Lugh, so I pray to all of them daily. I pray to Cernunnos and the Morrígan as part of the weekly devotions they have each requested of me. I pray to Ma'at daily, both as a representative of the Neteru (the gods of Egypt) as a whole and as a goddess of justice and order. I have looser relationships with numerous other deities. If the gods listed above are family who live in my house or perhaps down the street, this second category represents the relatives living far away whom I see once or twice a year. I pray to them on occasion. And when I'm preparing for a group ritual, I will pray to the deities of the occasion whether I know them or not. I occasionally pray to unknown deities on behalf of a friend who follows them.

Having said all that, if you don't know who to pray to, just pray. And then listen.

A Methodist minister once told me most people he counseled treat prayer like a spare tire. They keep it locked in the trunk of their cars and ignore it until they have an emergency. Then they dig it out and hope it has enough air in it to get them home. Like all spiritual practices, prayer works best when you work at it on a regular basis. Write or find a prayer you can say every day at the same time. It doesn't have to be long; in many ways it's better if it isn't. My morning prayers are extremely short because getting up in the morning is hard enough as it is. Next, make a commitment to pray that prayer every day. If you forget one day, pick it up again the next day. If you need reminders or prompts, prayer beads work very well.

Writing in *De Mysteriis* [On the Mysteries] in about 300 CE, the Greek Neoplatonist Iamblichus said: "It remains, therefore, at the end of this discourse, for me to pray to the gods to grant both to me and to you the unalterable preservation of true thoughts, to implant in us the truth of eternal things forever, and to grant to us a participation in the more perfect conceptions of the gods in which the most blessed end of good things is placed before us, along with the sanction of the harmonious friendship between us."

May it be so.

PRAY FOR THE DEAD

On October 1, 2017, a man opened fire on a crowd of concert-goers in Las Vegas. Fifty-eight people were killed and more than eight hundred were injured. My first response was, "Pray for the dead. The living won't listen." It was an expression of frustration at yet another mass shooting in a country that accepts them as inevitable. It was also genuine concern for the fifty-eight people who died a sudden and violent death.

Some traditions teach that your state of mind at death determines (or at least, strongly influences) your position in the afterlife and in the next life … or if you even get to the afterlife. Some of the most famous ghosts are connected to people who died tragically. Whether those ghosts are earthbound spirits or simply energetic "remains" is another question for another time (my best guess: sometimes it's one, sometimes it's the other). In any case, dying in pain, fear, and anger is hardly conducive to peacefully moving on to whatever comes next. The dead deserve our prayers and offerings for a smooth transition.

Growing up in a fundamentalist church, I was taught that prayers for the dead were useless, that it was "too late" to pray for them. According to fundamentalist doctrine, the dead were immediately either in heaven or in hell and nothing could be done to change their fate. I do my best to avoid critiquing the doctrines of other religions, as we have all different foundational assumptions, values, and ways of interacting with the world. Really, we have no common ground to debate the nature of the afterlife or the status of those who have died. But the reason prayers for the dead are considered useless in our mainstream culture is due to the prominence of Protestant Christianity in the United States. This is blasphemy, the act of speaking sacrilegiously about sacred things.

Most of my complaints against fundamentalism deal with facts: the bible is not the inerrant word of god, the Earth is far more than six thousand years old, and apocalyptic prophecies have a 3,500-year track record of being wrong every single time. Some of my complaints deal with outcomes: teaching small children that failing to follow your religion will send them into eternal torment can cause anxiety to a degree that can properly be classified as child abuse.

Blasphemy is a religious charge, not a factual one. It is a charge that is ripe for exploitation (as with the fundamentalist Muslim governments who occasionally imprison people for blasphemy against Islam) and therefore should never carry a secular penalty. Yet the concept remains in our vocabulary because some things are so sacred that to profane them demands a response.

Not much is as sacred as the dead, so saying it's too late abandons them to deal with being dead on their own, needlessly severing a relationship that death has altered but has not ended. We must do better for the dead.

Another blasphemy I hear at times like these goes, "Funerals are for the living." Yes, funerals *are* a necessity for the living. They're rites of passage that allow people to process their grief and collectively understand that the deceased is no longer with them. The relationship has shifted from one of family member or friend to one of ancestor or beloved dead. Funerals tell the survivors that they've done what needed to be done for the dead and now it's OK for regular life to resume.

What's unfortunate is that many funerals do not do what needs to be done for the dead. The good ones celebrate the life of the recently deceased. The bad ones serve as an excuse for preaching threats of hellfire to the grieving and vulnerable. Precious few actually address the needs of the dead.

Many traditions teach that the dead do not immediately move on to the Otherworld but instead hang around for a few days or weeks. Some have to figure out they're dead (think Bruce Willis in *The Sixth Sense*). Some are reluctant to leave their loved ones. Some have unfinished business, particularly those who died sudden and violent deaths. Good funerals tell the dead, "We loved you, we still love you, we will miss you, but we will be OK." They say, "It's OK to move on." They call the person's ancestors and deities to serve as psychopomps to assist them in the crossing.

Our species has always buried our dead with grave goods, and to this day some cultures and traditions still follow specific rites and requirements, such as preparing the body in a certain way or giving the dead coins or other precious items to pay a ferryman. Our most ancient ancestors were not that different from us—they would not have buried perfectly good tools, jewelry, and other items unless they thought it was necessary. The world's many funerary customs are far beyond the scope of this book; I encourage you to research the requirements of your tradition before there is a need to conduct a funeral. And whatever your tradition may be, there are things the living must do for the dead.

It is your responsibility to pray for your dead. Your prayers help your family member or other loved one to begin the process of transitioning from "recently deceased" to "beloved ancestor." They have their hands full dealing with their new circumstances—the sooner they move on, the sooner they can become an ancestral ally who can help you here and now.

Failure to help the dead move on can have consequences for the living beyond the stereotypical hauntings and such. A few years ago, I came across someone stuck living painfully in this world years after their time because the long-dead ancestor who needed to help them cross was stuck themselves. After proper rites were performed for the ancestor, all quickly became as it should be.

Praying for the dead is sacred work. Abandoning the dead is blasphemy.

MEDITATION: A PAGAN APPROACH

I have two interrelated definitions of meditation: it is reflection, contemplation, and focusing thoughts on a single point. It is also listening, especially when we listen for the presence of the gods and spirits.

Most of us are familiar with mindfulness meditation. This is the meditation our Buddhist friends teach and that has caught on with people of all religions. Simply sit and focus your attention on your breathing. That's all. When your mind starts to wander, gently bring your focus back to your breath. Some traditions place importance on proper posture. Some say the goal is to empty the mind, while others say the goal is simply to sit. As a Pagan, I'm less concerned about

Buddhist thoughts about meditation than I am about learning Buddhist techniques for meditation.

The benefits of mindfulness meditation are many and verifiable. It can lower blood pressure, reduce stress and depression (though it is not a panacea), and there is evidence it can improve overall brain health. Mainly, it trains the mind to ignore distractions and focus only on the task at hand. This skill is extremely helpful in other spiritual practices. It's also a difficult skill to cultivate. It's not like riding a bicycle, where once you've got it, you've got it for life. The "monkey mind" is always there, eager to latch on to the next shiny distraction. Mindfulness meditation requires constant practice.

More frequently I practice contemplative meditation. Here we're still trying to focus our attention on just one thing, but instead of the breath we're focusing on a concept, an ideal, or a person—in particular, the person of a deity.

I find it easiest to meditate in a darkened room. The dark hides many this-world distractions and makes it easier to focus on Otherworldly persons and what they have to say. I usually sit on the floor, in part because that's what I learned from Buddhist meditation classes, but also because it's convenient. However, as I get older, I find that some days it's difficult to sit on the floor. On those days I sit in a chair instead.

If I'm going to meditate on a deity, I'll place their statue or other representation in front of me. I light just enough candles to see the image clearly, usually one candle is enough. I begin with a couple of deep breaths to relax, and then I offer a prayer of invocation:

"Cernunnos, Lord of the Animals and Lord of the Hunt, God of the Forest and of Green Growing Things, I ask you to join me here and bless me with your presence. Great Hunter and Hunted, be welcome here."

If I'm doing this as part of a larger devotional ritual I'll make offerings here. If this is just a meditation, this is the extent of my invocation.

And then I sit, gaze at the statue, and contemplate the deity of the occasion. In the case of Cernunnos, I may begin by concentrating on a mighty stag or a man with antlers on his head. Unlike mindfulness meditation where the goal is to empty the mind or to keep it focused solely on the breath, in this meditation I let my mind go where it will but only within the limits of the object of the meditation. If I'm meditating on Cernunnos and I start to see a forest, I explore the forest. If an animal catches my attention, I watch it. I may smell the air, feel the wind, or drink the water. If my mind starts to wander from drinking water to drinking wine to the bottle of wine I want to pick up next time I'm out, then I bring my focus back to the statue and back to Cernunnos and all the virtues, values, and persons associated with him.

This same technique works very well in nature. Instead of using a statue or other image, go outside and focus on a tree, rock, the moon, or a star. These meditations tend to be shorter than indoor sitting meditations. You can only stand looking up at the moon for so long before your neck or back or legs start to become an unavoidable distraction, and that's okay. I've had some amazing experiences of the night sky that lasted less than a minute and some that lasted much longer. If you're watching the sunrise or sunset, it's fine to move around a bit. It's also fine to sit in a chair and take in the whole landscape.

Some of the most powerful nature meditations involve trees. Find a suitable tree, introduce yourself, and ask if the tree would like to speak with you. If you get a positive response (you'll feel it, not hear it), sit on the ground with your back resting on the trunk of the tree. Now contemplate the tree, its roots and branches, the sap flowing through it, and the creatures living in it. See what it sees, feel what it feels. Listen. Don't expect the tree to "teach" you anything. Trees are persons who do their own things for their own reasons—they're not here to serve humans. But like all persons, we can form relationships with them that when done right are beneficial to both parties.

Walking meditation is my favorite and most frequent form of meditation. It can be devotional, contemplative, or even mindful. It's done while walking outdoors (there are some who can even do walking meditation on a treadmill). I exercise before work most weekday mornings. Because of the hours of my job, that means I'm usually outdoors before dawn, although it starts to get light before I'm done. There is something magical about beginning a meditation in darkness and finishing in light—liminal zones are powerful times.

Some of my best writing is done while walking. Is that meditation? Not exactly, but the process is very similar. As with the contemplative meditation, I let my mind go where it will within the boundaries of the topic at hand. If it starts to wander into the upcoming work day or next month's vacation, I bring it back to what I'm trying to write about.

Mindfulness meditation builds skills in focusing. Contemplative meditation builds skills in listening. Contemplate a deity and you will inevitably begin with the things you know about them: Cernunnos is a god of the animals. Continue the contemplation and you will start to realize that the things you know carry implications: if I'm devoted to a god of the animals, then I should make sure my home is welcoming to animals or at least not hostile to them. These implications can be many and deep.

After a while, contemplation morphs into listening. Now you "hear" things that are neither your thoughts nor the implications of your thoughts. Now you "hear" the voices of others. That always raises the question of how you know which thoughts are yours and which thoughts are communication from someone else. The first clue comes from the Temple of Apollo at Delphi: know thyself. If you know yourself well, it's fairly easy to know which thoughts are yours and which aren't. Compare what you hear with what's known about the god, ancestor, or spirit talking to you—is it "in character" for them? Compare it with what other practitioners are hearing—let UPG (unverified personal gnosis) become SPG (shared personal gnosis). Pull out your favorite divination tool—or better yet, contact an experienced diviner.

Are you still unsure who or what you're hearing from? Then don't worry about the source and concentrate on the message. What are you hearing? Does it make good sense? Is it in alignment with your values and your ethics? Then just do it.

Meditation is most commonly associated with Buddhism but is practiced in every religion and occasionally by people with no religion. Its regular practice has demonstrable benefits, and it builds the skills necessary for many spiritual experiences.

DEVOTIONAL READING

In a speech to the Society of the Adelphi in Maine in 1841, Ralph Waldo Emerson said, "a man will worship something … That which dominates will determine his life and character. Therefore it behooves us to be careful what we worship, for what we are worshipping we are becoming."

One of the ways we become more like our gods is through devotion. And one of the simplest and most effective forms of devotion is reading. Now, not just any reading will suffice—the more fact-based academic study type is of limited benefit here. Devotional reading requires poetry, stories, and myths. It requires hymns and anthems. It needs word-pictures that reach into our souls and stoke the fires of inspiration.

We have some devotional material from our ancient ancestors, though more in some traditions than in others. There are the classic myths of the Greeks and Romans, the Norse Edda, and the Welsh Mabinogi. There are the hymns of Orpheus, translated into English and available for free on the internet. And there are newer translations and interpretations of the classics, some of which are done by Pagans that do not carry the monotheist assumptions and prejudices of the English translators of the nineteenth and twentieth centuries. Whatever your

Pagan tradition, there is almost certainly some material available for devotional use.

There are also modern works of devotion. Most are small, self-published anthologies dedicated to a specific deity. Several are listed in the bibliography, but there are others, and more are being created all the time. As well, there's a wealth of devotional poetry on the internet. The quality varies from volume to volume and from piece to piece, but there's almost certainly something out there that will speak to you.

There are two things to do with devotional material once you find it. The first is simply to read it, slowly and carefully … and in small bites. Take one story or one hymn at a time. The goal isn't to scan through and pick up the high points—the goal is to absorb it, to internalize it.

Read it. Then read it again. Then set the book down and contemplate what you read. Don't analyze it; simply let your thoughts go where they will. Meditate on the character of the deities in the piece. Meditate on their virtues and their actions. At some point you will want to think about how you can be more like them, but for now—for the length of the devotion—simply let the words and concepts sink into your soul.

The second thing you can do with devotional material is to perform it. Hymns are meant to be sung, after all. And for ancient hymns that don't have tunes, perhaps you can make one up. I'm personally not very good at that, so I read hymns aloud like a poetry performance. Stand before your altar and speak words of devotion to your gods.

As much fun as filking tunes can be—and despite the many amusing Pagan verses people have written for "Give Me That Old Time Religion"—I do not recommend setting Pagan hymns to Christian tunes. The tunes themselves have Christian associations that can be difficult for those who are trying to make a clean break with a religion that was troubling to them. That said, some Christian hymns are set to folk songs that likely have Pagan roots. Those are good for reclaiming if you can focus on the roots and not on the more recent associations.

If you use the same devotional words frequently, you'll find you no longer need the printed text: you'll start to memorize them. You may also find yourself making changes based on your own experiences and understanding. While I'm reluctant to edit the words of the ancients, remember that you're working with someone else's translation that may or may not align with the intent of the original authors. Do it if it works, but if you publish your revision (even on social media), be sure to credit the original writer and translator and note what you've changed.

Maintain your practice long enough and you may find new words of devotion coming to you. Your own composition is a powerful offering to your gods. Just remember that the primary goal remains devotion to our gods and their virtues and values. Devotional reading helps us reinforce that in our hearts and minds.

OFFERINGS

I suspect early Wiccans wanted to insulate themselves against mindless and fearful accusations of animal or even human sacrifice, as the Charge of the Goddess says, "Nor do I demand aught of sacrifice, for behold: I am the Mother of all things and my love is poured upon the earth." Offerings were quite common in ancient times, however, and a growing number of Pagans (especially polytheists) have revived the practice. Giving things to the gods, ancestors, and other spirits is a regular part of our spiritual practice. Although the practice of offerings and sacrifices is not universal among modern Pagans, it's a worthwhile topic.

What's the difference between an offering and a sacrifice? While the two terms have different word origins and definitions (offerings are given while sacrifices refer to things made sacred), in contemporary practice they're virtually the same. I joke that pouring wine is an offering but pouring my favorite local stout is a sacrifice.

Offerings generally (but not exclusively) take the form of food and drink: wine, beer, mead, or whiskey; grain, bread, meat, or sweets. It can take the form of money, objects, or service. It can take other forms as required by tradition or by the gods themselves.

If you're new to polytheism, especially if you come from a Protestant or an atheist background where religion is all about beliefs, dogma, and the written word, the idea of offerings may strike you as odd, anachronistic, or unnecessary. But for many, offerings are the cornerstone of our religious practice.

Offerings are made to express hospitality. If you invited a friend over to your house, you'd offer them something to drink as soon as they arrived. If they were there a while or showed up at dinner time, you'd offer them something to eat. You'd try to be a good, generous, thoughtful host who cares for their guests. The same is true with our interactions with the gods. We don't want to invite them to our rituals and start demanding they give us stuff; we want to be polite and generous. We make offerings to the gods to show our respect for them and demonstrate that we practice the virtue of hospitality.

Offerings are made to promote reciprocity. The world runs on reciprocity: "I give so that you may give." Sometimes the offering is quid pro quo, like a gift for a gift or payment for a service. As in real life, sometimes you don't expect to be paid back right away. If you do a favor for a friend, you know that someday they'll do something for you. Occasionally the reciprocity is even less structured—perhaps you do a good deed and figure things will even out in the long run. We give to the gods so the gods will give to us. What we're doing isn't appeasement, nor is it bribery…as if a divine being could be bribed with a glass of wine! What we're doing is demonstrating that we understand the world runs on honest exchange.

Offerings are made because our ancestors made offerings. Contemporary polytheists aren't building a religion from scratch. We're reviving, restoring, and reimagining the religions of our ancestors. We need not—and should not—slavishly duplicate everything they believed and did, but where a practice was meaningful and helpful to the ancients, we are foolish if we do not at least explore it. Reviving their practices not only lets us learn from them, it also helps restore the bonds across generations as we do now what they did then.

Offerings are made because the gods ask for offerings. If a good friend asks me for something, my first impulse is to say yes. Sometimes it's as simple as a god saying, "I want that." Sometimes there's a practical reason they want it. Sometimes there's a whimsical (to us) reason. Sometimes there's no reason at all, just that familiar voice or feeling or intuition that they want something from us. I've learned to trust that if they ask for something, the best thing to do is give it to them. There are limits, of course. I grew up hearing the story of Abraham almost sacrificing his son Isaac to Yahweh. If that was a test, Abraham failed. I've never been asked to give something I felt I shouldn't give or had no right to give.

Offerings are made to remind ourselves that we have enough. As the meme I occasionally see on Facebook says, you can't pour from an empty cup—you can't give what you don't have. By historical standards, however, all but the poorest among us have far more than we truly need. Offerings and sacrifices remind us that we are not lessened when we give. We can and should debate how much we should give, who we should give to, and how our gifts should be made. But as we give to the gods, we are reminded that we can also give to our fellow humans because we have enough.

Offerings are made to remind ourselves to do what must be done. If I'm honest, I love being hospitable to the gods and giving them what they ask for, but at the end of the day I really don't like pouring out perfectly good wine I could drink. I also don't like going to work every day, wearing glasses, and putting up with Texas summers, *but* I do all these things because they must be done. They are necessary if I'm going to make enough money to live the way I want to live, if I want to read anything smaller than 16-point type, and if I want to enjoy the mild Texas winters and low cost of living. When I make offerings, I'm reminded that nothing comes for free. Even the most priceless choices involve a trade-off of one thing or another: if I give a rare bottle of wine to the gods, I cannot give it to a friend. We do what must be done, such is life.

Offerings are made to express devotion. Why do we send flowers to a spouse, bring souvenirs back for family, or take a close friend out for an expensive dinner? Because we love them and want to do something nice and thoughtful for them. In other words, we want to express our devotion to them. Likewise, as we come to know the gods and understand their power and virtue, we not only want to ally ourselves by working for their causes, we also want to express our devotion to them. We make offerings because we want them to enjoy what we have to give, however ultimately insignificant that may be.

I encourage you to make offerings a regular part of your spiritual practice, and especially part of your usual ritual liturgy. If you call (invite, invoke) a being into your ritual, be a good host and offer food and drink. Practice good hospitality, reciprocity, and devotion with all your guests.

BECAUSE YOU'RE NOT A BEGINNER ANYMORE

Devotional practice is covered in *The Path of Paganism,* and I blog about it regularly. Yet here we are, talking about it again. Why cover the basics yet again? Because they're that important.

All-star basketball players practice free throw shooting every day. Concert pianists practice several hours every day. The Dalai Lama meditates four hours every day. Masters of any art don't learn the basics and then move on. They keep practicing the basics day after day, year after year. Whatever you're doing now, do it more—more frequently and for longer periods of time. If there are practices you're not doing, pick them up at least on a trial basis. How much is necessary? That depends on what you're called to do. Most of us with jobs and school and families can't spend four hours on spiritual practice every day—I certainly can't, and that's okay. A little more practice will make you a better polytheist. Most of us aren't called to become the Pagan equivalent of the Dalai Lama, but if that is your calling, that's the level of commitment required.

Polytheist religions are religions of the gods, but they are rooted in places and cultures. If you worship Celtic gods, you need to understand Celtic history and culture. I've read books on the history of Ireland, Scotland, and Wales. I've read translations of ancient stories. I've been to all three countries (which, to be clear, aren't the extent of the Celtic world). I've walked the land and experienced some of the ancient sites. The fact that some of my ancestors came to America from Ireland two-hundred and twenty years ago is of little importance. I'm an American; no amount of study and travel is ever going to make me Irish, but this isn't about becoming Irish. It's about learning how the gods of Ireland were understood and worshipped in the past and providing context for our understanding and worship of them here and now.

We have stories about the Celtic deities, but they weren't written down till well into the Christian era. We know much less about their stories and worship than we know about, say, the Greeks. Where we have missing information, we can study the beliefs and practices of better documented neighbors. A lot of intermediate polytheism looks like mundane academic study. What we learn becomes the "frog DNA" (to borrow from *Jurassic Park*) in our practices. Sometimes it works and sometimes it doesn't, but it gives us a good place to start.

Prayer—talking to the gods—is important, as is listening to them. Who is speaking to you? What are they calling you to do? Perhaps they're calling you to priesthood, but don't jump to that conclusion. Priesthood is a specific set of duties and commitments that often looks very different from what Catholic priests and Protestant ministers do.

There are many forms of service, and priesthood is only one. Listen for what you're being called to do. That may take months or even years. Keep listening. When you hear something, confirm it with divination.

What training does your faith require? What study? Do you need a teacher? If so, where can you find one? A quote often misattributed to the Buddha goes, "When the student is ready, the teacher will appear." Sometimes that's true, but teachers tend to appear when you hang out in places where teachers teach on a regular basis. Maybe you don't need training at all—perhaps you just need to get to work. Learning by doing is a vastly underrated form of education.

Go far enough and eventually you'll run out of teachers. But there are always people who are knowledgeable and experienced who can serve as sounding boards, sanity checks, and general resources on topics you're still learning. There are several of these people in my life, and I'm thankful for all of them.

As you grow in depth and move from beginner to intermediate, consistency and reliability become of greater and greater importance. When you're first starting out, you're going to make mistakes. You're going to forget things. You may even consciously make a bad decision. Rarely are there serious repercussions. While obviously I cannot speak for all the gods, the ones I've worked with have been nothing like the god of the Old Testament, looking to smite people for the slightest slip-up. As your practice deepens, however, expectations get more serious. The Morrígan asked me for weekly offerings. When I went on vacation a month later, I wondered about my usual obligations. I heard in response "every week—period," so I've poured libations into a river in Ireland and into decorative shrubbery in Las Vegas. At some point, "I was too busy" is no longer a valid excuse. You have daily obligations and you meet them, no matter how busy, tired, or uninspired you are.

As your devotional relationship develops, you can try things out, see how they go, and see what responses you get. There are no obligations for either party (obviously, if you're one of the few who find yourself forcefully claimed, this doesn't apply to you—I'm genuinely sorry). Do this for long enough, however, and it is likely you will be asked for an oath. Oaths may be for a fixed period of time: a month or a year or a decade. They may be for life. I know some people who've sworn oaths for "this life and beyond"—I'm not doing that; I don't know what the next life is going to look like and will deal with it when I get there. Remember that you can negotiate terms and you can say no . . . unless you can't. If you haven't been there, it's hard to explain. Most deities don't bother with reluctant devotees; they usually move on and find someone else who's more agreeable, but not always. Keep going deeper into your devotion and your polytheist practice, and you'll be asked to go deeper still.

This level of devotion and worship isn't for everyone, and neither should this type of practice be considered normative for all polytheists. There is or should be a place in our polytheist religions and traditions for people who just want to honor the gods and live an ordinary life. Our movement needs accountants and auto mechanics as much as it needs priests and mystics. But if you've begun a polytheist practice and have found it meaningful and helpful, I encourage you to go deeper: move beyond Polytheism 101. Come on in . . . the water's fine.

6

MAGICAL PRACTICE

ALEISTER CROWLEY'S CLASSIC DEFINITION of magic is "the science and art of causing change to occur in conformity with will." Using that definition (or pretty much any other common definition), most religions are full of magic.

Judaism has the Passover story of blood over the doorposts and Moses parting the Red Sea. Christianity has the miracles of Jesus and the apostles, transubstantiation, and the forgiveness of sins. We don't know much about ancient Druidry, but there are numerous references to Druid magic in the historic and literary records, including shapeshifting. Even the nontheistic versions of Buddhism speak of the changes in consciousness produced by mindfulness and meditation.

Religion has always had an uneasy relationship with magic. Religion (from the Latin *religare*: "to bind together") is largely a group thing where common beliefs and common practices maintain social order and good relationships with the gods and spirits. Magic is powerful; individuals may use it for personal gain in ways that harm the common good, to harm those who have wronged or slighted them, or to subvert authority. Most of us know the Old Testament prescribes death for the malicious use of magic, but it may surprise you to know that Roman law did as well. Even today, there are places in the world where those suspected of witchcraft are regularly executed. Despite these concerns, most religions have a tradition of magic within them. Sometimes it's considered acceptable for especially holy people to study magic. More frequently, ordinary people just do it because they have a need for it.

Knowing all these things, we're left with the question: what is or what should be magic's place in our contemporary polytheist religions and traditions?

Some polytheists ignore magic, preferring to focus on devotion to the gods, ancestors, and spirits. Some think magic is an impious attempt to usurp power that rightfully belongs to the gods. I came to polytheism through the modern Pagan movement with its strong emphasis on magic and witchcraft. Having learned a few things along the way, I'm not inclined to give them up. Every other religion has a tradition of magic within it, whether that tradition is official, unacknowledged, or actively opposed by orthodox leadership. And given the general decline of the wider world, our need for magic grows stronger every day.

I say magic is part of our heritage. Let's embrace it: let's study it, learn it, practice it, and teach it. Let's incorporate it into our private practices and our group workings. Let's incorporate it into our public rituals and celebrations, at least to the extent we can do so responsibly. Those old fears of witchcraft aren't entirely unfounded—some people can't be trusted with magic. And some people can't or don't want to deal with the risks involved in serious magic. But magic is part of our legacy, and we do ourselves no favors if we reject it.

Each polytheist religion and each individual polytheist must make their own decision as to the place of magic in their tradition and practice. The polytheism I practice, teach, and advocate for includes magic.

There are four basic categories of magic I work with: theurgy, energy magic, traditional witchcraft, and sigil magic.

Theurgy ("god-working") is magic done through or with the assistance of divine beings. Sometimes this is a simple intercessory prayer such as asking a deity for a blessing or assistance. Other times it involves invoking or meditating on a god or spirit in order to absorb some of their divine essence and become more godlike yourself. This is a worthy goal, and there are numerous groups and traditions that teach this practice, many that are part of the Western Mystery Tradition. Polytheist theurgy is grounded in respectful reciprocal relationships, not on discovering your true self (a good and necessary goal but neither theurgy nor polytheism).

Energy magic is the psychic manipulation of power for everything from grounding and centering to shielding to stopping a Nazi invasion, as with Operation Cone of Power in World War II, reported by Gerald Gardner and Dion Fortune. Sometimes it involves drawing power up from the earth and down from the sky. Other times it involves raising power through dancing, chanting, drumming, or other activities, and then releasing it toward a target, like in a typical Wiccan ritual. Energy magic is simple and intuitive, in large part because of its many parallels in fiction and popular culture. Don't expect to ever see sparks shooting from your fingertips but do the work and you'll be able to feel the energy moving through you.

Some grimoire magicians have criticized energy magic's authenticity, claiming it was unheard of prior to the early twentieth century... which coincidentally was when electricity and radio became commonplace. That may be true, but I've used it successfully enough times that its origin isn't really important any more. It works, and that's all that matters.

Traditional witchcraft is quite popular these days, and its exact boundaries are rather unclear. Here I'm referring to home remedies, dowsing, poppets, candle magic, herb magic, and general kitchen witchery. It's the magic of the cunning men and women of Britain and Ireland and their Appalachian relatives. It is largely (but not entirely) sympathetic magic based on associations and correspondences ("this is like that, therefore this will influence that"). It is secular in nature but is frequently wrapped up in Christian references and imagery because the people practicing it have been Christians.

Sigil magic is my favorite tool for magical workings. It's the graphical process of writing your goal, converting it from an English (or your language of choice) sentence into a visual glyph, activating the sigil, then letting it go. It's simple, straightforward, and effective. Gordon White's book *The Chaos Protocols* is the best introduction I know.

The variety of practices outlined here are not the only forms of magic, but they're the forms I use in my practice. Other than theurgy, they have little if anything to do with the religious regard for many real gods. They aren't part of polytheism, much less one of its requirements. However, magic has been a part of religion since the beginnings of religion and is part of the polytheist religion I practice. Magic is our legacy, one we would do well to reclaim and relearn.

HOW MAGIC WORKS

Regardless of which form of magic you use, one basic question remains: how does it work? For most of us, that question is less important than how we make magic work. If we can do the spells and get the results, does it really matter how it happened? For the forever curious who may want to get past someone else's cookbook spells to start doing their own magic, some idea is required of what's going on when circles are cast, candles are lit, and incantations are chanted.

Personally speaking, I came to a three-fold understanding of how magic works very early on my Pagan journey; in the more than twenty years since, I've had countless magical successes as well as my share of failures. I've studied magic and religion in great depth and have had experiences that have rearranged my understanding of the world and what is and isn't possible. My theology has changed, my philosophy has changed, and my practice has changed. The way I understand magic has remained constant, however, because I've yet to find a better model for how magic works.

Defining magic is hard. There's a bit of "I know it when I see it" involved. As Crowley said, magic is a science and an art; it's about creating change; it involves intent and will. It doesn't attempt to draw a bright line between ordinary efforts and Otherworldly efforts—all those lines usually accomplish is getting in the way.

A few years ago, I was teaching a magic class. Before the first meeting, there was the usual socializing and chatting. When the starting time came, I sat down, pulled out a piece of paper, and wrote "quiet please" on it. I held the paper up, and people gradually noticed and stopped talking. After a few seconds of silence, I said, "Look what I just did. I drew some lines on a sheet of paper and the room got quiet. You've just seen an example of successful magic." Not all magic is that simple or that ordinary, but mastering simple and ordinary magic definitely opens our eyes to deeper and more complex magic. And here also is a reminder of the most important criteria in evaluating magic: regardless of the means and methods, did it work or not? When we examine what works, we start to notice that things tend to fall into three broad categories.

MAGIC WORKS THROUGH THE INTERCESSION OF GODS AND SPIRITS

I occasionally hear people say that magic is just like prayer. There's usually an undercurrent of "please don't be afraid of me" involved here, but there's some truth to it. Sometimes magic is just like prayer. We ask a god, ancestor, or some other spirit to do something for us, and they do.

My relationship with the Morrígan began this way—I asked for her help and she responded. After the third time, she said, "I have done this for you. Now I want you to do something for me."

Both believers and skeptics can point to studies on the efficacy of prayer that support their views. I've seen enough first-hand results over the years to convince me. Intercessory prayer may not always give us what we want (or even what we ask for), but it has an impact on our lives.

Why would gods or spirits grant our requests? What's in it for them? Sometimes they're in agreement with us, wanting what we want. My early prayers to the Morrígan were for protection for friends in distant places who were in physical danger, well within the scope of interest for a battle goddess. We had a common interest, I brought a need to her attention, and she chose to act. Other times, a transaction is involved—reciprocity makes the world go around. A spirit agrees to give us information or to open the way in exchange for certain offerings. A god agrees to do something for us but wants our service in return. There are as many "hows" and "whys" as there are spirits and people.

Of course, sometimes prayer is a little of both. Did the Morrígan grant my prayers because she was in alignment with my requests or because she saw the opportunity to pull a Druid into her long-term service? I honestly don't know. The gods have many virtues, but transparency is not one of them, especially when it comes to the Great Queen.

MAGIC WORKS THROUGH THE MANIPULATION OF UNSEEN FORCES

We sit in meditation, extend roots into the ground, and draw up energy from the earth. We extend branches into the sky and draw down energy from the sun and moon. We dance and chant around a circle, raising energy higher and higher until we open the circle and send our energy into the universe to do our work. We feel threatened, so we use some of our own energy to shield ourselves from harm.

What is this energy? It's not electromagnetic energy like sunlight and radio waves. It's no coincidence that the idea of magical energy first arose during the late nineteenth and early twentieth centuries when electric lights and later radio and television transmissions became commonplace. The differences haven't always been well articulated. Bad science makes for bad religion … and bad magic. Sometimes the power comes from us, while other times we're merely the conduit for the power of others. Whatever these unseen forces are, there are ways we can manipulate them whether by raising and directing them or by more subtle methods.

MAGIC WORKS THROUGH PSYCHOLOGICAL PROGRAMMING

Some magic requires no Otherworldly assistance and no unexplainable forces. Some magic is plain old psychological programming.

Put yourself in a receptive state of mind. Plant ideas, not with words that require conscious translation but with symbols that communicate directly with your subconscious … the part of your brain that runs most of the show anyway. Reinforce it with chanting, dancing, singing, or other actions. Do it all in a setting that looks and feels so different from the ordinary world that you resist the urge to kill it with deconstruction and analysis. Before long, those ideas you planted start to sprout and bear fruit in the ordinary world. You start behaving differently. You start eating differently. You stop biting your fingernails (I've done this one successfully several times, though it only seems to last for a couple months). You start putting yourself in situations where you can find a job, or a house, or a lover, or a friend … and eventually you get what you worked for. Your world starts to change.

Changing habits is very hard. Doing a spell once won't be enough; even if you have an initial success, you'll probably need to work it again and again. That's okay.

Is it proper to call this magic? If it works, does it really matter?

SOMETIMES IT'S ONE, SOMETIMES IT'S TWO, SOMETIMES IT'S ALL THREE

Magic is many things, but one thing it is not is easy. If you can get what you want through ordinary effort, do it. Working magic doesn't make something happen; it improves the odds that it will happen. If you can just go do it, that raises the odds to 100 percent. If you can't just do it on your own, you need magic. And if it's important enough to work magic, it's important enough to work magic in all three ways. Raise and direct energy toward your goal. Work sigil magic. Do visualizations. Pray to your gods for help. Make offerings to your ancestors for their assistance. Call on a relevant spirit. And do all this in a way that speaks to your subconscious with sights and sounds and smells.

Overanalyzing something can kill the magic. Do your working and then let it go. The good news is that belief is irrelevant. If you do the magic properly, you'll get the results whether you "believe in" magic or not. The best way to believe in magic is to work magic.

Our understanding of how anything works has a direct impact on how we can make use of it. If we believe magic is only spirits or only unseen forces or only psychological programming, we will only use that portion and ignore other magic that is also available to us. This three-fold understanding of magic has given me the foundation to work the magic I need.

THE MAGIC OF WILD PLACES

For all that Paganism is a religion of nature, most Pagans live in urban and suburban environments. We're thus quick to point out that "we're part of nature too" and "nature is everywhere"—statements that are true both physically and spiritually. Our Pagan practices help insure that our residence in human-built and human-dominated spaces does not disconnect us from nature. Nature is everywhere, but there's still something special about wild places.

I grew up with the woods literally twenty feet outside my back door. When I was very small and before subdivisions started crowding in, the woods seemed boundless. Even though I knew that if I walked far enough I'd eventually run into a well-known road, the woods were deep enough that they never became completely familiar. Years later, when I read the Celtic stories of hunters chasing animals into the woods and suddenly finding themselves in Otherworldly territory, I had no trouble relating.

I never got lost in the woods in part because I have a good sense of direction and in part because our woods just weren't that big. There were many times I found an interesting spot and enjoyed a few minutes or even a few hours there, but was unable to find it again when I went back. Did I wander into the Otherworld on some of those expeditions? The thought never occurred to me at the time, but when I look back on my experiences, I think it's likely that happened at least once or twice. I would not be a Pagan without the woods. Or more precisely, I would not be the kind of Pagan I am without my experiences of the wild, both in the woods where I grew up and in other wild places I've visited in the years since I left home. There is magic in wild places.

The wild is a place of refuge. For most people, this statement may seem nonsensical. The wild is unpredictable and dangerous: it has plants that will poison you, animals that will eat you, and weather that will drown, freeze, or burn you. But it is in those very dangers that the safety of the wild can be found—they scare people away.

When I needed a quiet place, the woods were there. When I needed to get away from troublesome people, the woods were there. I never felt like I was hiding, only disappearing to somewhere else. Part of American lore is the frontiersman, the person who, when civilization began encroaching, picked up and moved farther into the wild. Whether the details of that lore are historical isn't the point. Humans have been moving into the wild ever since our earliest ancestors left east Africa.

Dropping off the face of the earth is really hard to do in our modern era of electronic tracking, but retreating into the wild to avoid people is still possible. Even for those of us who like civilization, few things are as restorative as a trip to a remote place of natural beauty or a weekend camping in the woods.

The wild is a place of possibility. Food? Not much in the desert, but in other wild places there are roots, berries, nuts, and all kinds of wildlife. Materials to build a shelter? There are rocks, trees, leaves ... and caves in some places (but see who might already be living there first). Surviving in the wild isn't that difficult if you know how.

Making do in the wild for a few days is one thing. Living in the wild on an on-going basis is much harder. It takes a certain amount of knowledge, skills, and physical strength. It favors the young and the experienced, a rare combination. But for most of us, if we had to, we could. And knowing that we could live in the wild opens our minds to all kinds of possibilities. Suddenly, we realize we have more options than we think—there are ways to live other than working a meaningless job to make money to buy stuff we don't need and don't really want. Like the frontiersman, we know the alternatives to mainstream culture will be hard and risky, but they do exist. Realizing there are possibilities is the first step in changing our lives and our world.

The wild is full of spirits. The fairy tales I heard as a child were presented as fiction, so I assumed that's all they were. But everyone I knew accepted the possibility of ghosts, even if it didn't exactly square with the doctrines of their churches. Demons and other spirits were assumed to be real. Walk through the woods after dark and even someone as spiritually dense as I used to be could feel the presence of spiritual beings. Some of them are Otherworldly. Others are simply the spirits of the trees and rocks and animals who live there. When I think back on some of my experiences, I feel bad that I assumed everything I encountered was a malevolent spirit, but it was the only thing for which I had context. I'm now certain there was at least one nurturing spirit in those woods, plus a lot more that didn't give a damn about me one way or the other.

Go into the wild—even little pieces of the wild like parks and vacant lots, or an overgrown corner of your back yard. Go at night. Go by yourself. Block out the noise. Listen. What do you hear? What do you feel? Don't assume whatever is there is there for you—it is almost certainly not. Just learn to hear and see and feel what else—or who else—is out there. The wild is full of spirits.

It's necessary to be aware of your surroundings wherever you are, and malicious humans are far more dangerous than malicious spirits. Don't put yourself in needless danger.

If we stay too long in a wild place, it is our nature to domesticate it and civilize it, and then it is wild no more. My parents sold two thirds of the woods before I left for college that was turned into a subdivision. My mother sold the rest shortly after my father died. We owe it to future generations as well as to the physical and spiritual beings who live there now to preserve some wild places in perpetuity. We can also rewild places as we abandon them. Or rather, left alone, nature will reclaim them.

My Paganism, Druidry, and polytheism all have roots in the wild.

Blessed be the wild, for it is full of magic.

HOW DO YOU KNOW YOUR MAGIC WORKED?

Fictional magic can be entertaining and even inspiring, but it sets impossible expectations for real magic. The young witches and wizards of

Hogwarts struggled with *wingardium leviosa* wherein the feather either levitated or it didn't; they knew right away if their magic worked or not. Real magic is rarely as straightforward.

On one level it's simple: did you get what you enchanted for? Occasionally that can be answered yes or no. More often we see a bit of improvement here or there but not earth-shattering results. Remember that in most cases, magic doesn't actually cause anything to happen. Rather, magic makes it more likely that something will happen. You may do a great spell that would bring the result you want 99 times out of 100, but this was the one time it didn't work.

Further complicating things is the fact that most of us cast vague spells. A long time ago as an engineering student, I took a class called Contracts and Specifications that covered contract law for engineers. All I remember from that class was one day when the professor blared out, "You don't get what you want—you get what you write in the specs!" Anyone who's written specifications for programmers knows what I'm talking about. You can go over what you want, the programmer will come back with something for you to test, and you scream, "This wasn't what I wanted!" And then the programmer will point to the specifications and say, "But that's what you asked for." The program met the specs, so the programmer thinks it works. Figuring out if your magic worked is a process of comparing what you got against what you were trying to get.

What were you working for? Look at your spell. Pay great attention to your words—exactly *what* did you ask for? How might someone who doesn't live in your head interpret your words? Again: you don't get what you want, you get what you write in the specs.

If you got what you asked for and worked for, then your magic worked. If that's not what you really wanted, the problem isn't your magic. It's your target selection.

What did you really want? Did you ask for "money" when you needed $523.17? Did you enchant for "love" when you really wanted sex with a really attractive person…or maybe when you really wanted someone to overlook your perceived shortcomings? Did you cast a spell for a better job when you really wanted a deeper spiritual life?

If figuring out how to word a spell is hard, figuring out what you really want is three times harder. We all carry expectations that aren't our own, from family, friends, and society more generally. There's a whole industry dedicated to convincing us that we desperately need what they're selling. Figuring out what you want—and accepting that it's different from what you've always been told you're supposed to want—is hard. It's been hard since long before the ancient Greeks carved "Know Thyself" above the doors of the Temple of Apollo at Delphi. If you got what you enchanted for and the spell still feels like a failure, maybe you didn't enchant for what you really wanted.

There's something to be said for concentrating on the what and not worrying about the how. But if you can't describe the what, then you don't know what success looks like and you'll never know whether your magic worked or not. If you can't define success, your spell is probably too vague to be useful. Pick something smaller and more specific. We all want to be healthy, but what does "healthy" mean? Attaining a certain waist size? Avoiding heart disease and cancer? Never getting the flu? Being able to run marathons when you're seventy? Being able to travel when you're eighty? Some of these examples are realistic and some are not, but they're all different things. If you've never cared about being an athlete, being able to run or play tennis into your old age may not be important to you. If you've been a runner all your life, you may feel differently. "Healthy" means different things to different people.

If your magical working is too vague, pick something smaller and more specific. After you achieve that, see what you want to do next.

Keep records. Keep a magical diary—anything from a hand-bound book of parchment to a spiral notebook to a computer text file (my personal favorite). Different magical traditions have different protocols for record keeping: some want detailed records that would be at home in a science lab, while sigil magic says "fire it and forget it." At a minimum, write down what you worked for and when you should check up on it.

Obsessing over your spells and constantly checking for progress is a good way to kill the magic. There are various theories as to why that is—all I know is that it's true. The Witches Pyramid is to know, to will, to dare, and to keep silence, where the "keep silence" part applies to yourself as well as others. But do keep records—don't count on remembering everything you did and how you did it.

Never expect to convince your materialist friends. There is only one reason to keep records and review your results: so you can learn from both your successes and your failures and become a better magician. No amount of even well-documented success will change the mind of someone who is totally convinced there is no such thing as magic, and that's okay. Witches, Druids, and other magicians don't work magic to prove it can be done. We don't do it because it's easy. Mundane methods—no matter how laborious—are usually easier and always more certain than magical methods. We work magic because we have a great need and no other way to fulfill it.

PROGRESSIVE MAGIC

As a baby Pagan a long time ago, I was taught there are two kinds of magic: high magic, which is intended to refine the soul; and low magic, which is intended to get stuff done. Occultists did high magic, while witches did low magic. I never paid much attention to the classifications. Magic has always seemed like one thing to me. It has many different approaches and an infinite number of applications, but at the end of the day, magic is an attempt to move the odds in your favor. Whether you're trying to improve the odds of living a good and honorable life or if you're just trying to find a new job, you're basically doing the same thing.

The division of magic points toward a very real dilemma. On one hand, magic works best when it's focused and specific. On the other hand, many of the things we need magic to achieve are big and complicated. You may be the best magical archer in the world, but if you're facing the equivalent of a Roman legion, one perfectly placed arrow isn't going solve your problem. On top of that, many times you simply don't know what you want. You know what you think you want and what you've been told you're supposed to want, but will that make you happy? If a genie had granted me three wishes at age twenty-two, I would have set myself up to be rich, powerful . . . and miserable. I hadn't yet learned the concept of "enough."

The approach I've come to follow (albeit somewhat haphazardly) deals with this dilemma by breaking big problems and processes down into little ones that can be addressed with focused and specific actions both magical and mundane. It accepts that life is a long journey that includes some wrong turns, but it attempts to identify and correct those wrong turns as quickly as possible. I call this approach progressive magic. It has four main components.

CHOOSE A VISION

What do you want? What are you trying to accomplish? Where do you want to be, metaphorically or even literally? Recognizing you have a problem is the first step, but focusing only on what's wrong is likely to bring you more of what you don't want. What do you want to have or do or be instead? Many times, we don't know what we want because we don't know what's possible. So, read—history, religion, philosophy, and the social sciences. Fiction is fiction, but it can inspire us to make things real that weren't real before. Travel. If you can't travel, read the writings of those who have. There's a whole world out there; don't limit yourself to one little portion of it. Divination can help narrow your choices, and divination is especially good at showing you what things will look and feel like if you continue down a certain path.

When I first started on my Pagan journey, I wanted to be a Witch. Witchcraft and Wicca didn't work for me, but when I found Druidry, I knew this was it—I wanted to be a Druid. How do you go about becoming a Druid? I didn't know, but I knew it was my vision for the future. Progressive magic begins with a vision.

WORK ON TWO LEVELS

Our visions motivate us and keep us going when things get hard, so our visions need to be nurtured. We can nurture them via creative visualization, investigation and imagination, or even exploration. Keep your vision fixed firmly in your mind—this is our work on one level. Also remember that daydreams will get us nowhere unless we start doing something. You have to start somewhere, so pick something. If it's all new to you, pick something small and easy—early victories are important, no matter how small. Maybe this is something you can do with mundane effort. Maybe this is where you start the candle magic, herbal magic, or sigil magic. Maybe you do all three (hint: do all three).

In any case, pick something that's small enough that you can select a clear, focused target. For example, you can't go from being sedentary to running a marathon in a month. Assuming you are otherwise healthy, you can start walking and then move to running a short distance, and then a longer distance. You almost certainly can't topple the President of the United States, but you can influence specific appointments or legislation. Start taking steps toward your goal or chipping away at a big problem or building something new and better. Progressive magic takes things step by step, while keeping the ultimate goal in mind the whole time.

FAIL FAST

"Fail fast" is a current buzzy business term that's often misused. Let's be clear: failure is not the goal. The goal is instead to not let the fear of failure keep you from trying something new and different. And since you probably don't know exactly what you want and certainly don't know exactly how to get there, you will fail at least occasionally. The goal is to recognize your failures quickly and change course before it becomes too late or too expensive to change. Try not to make the same mistake twice, much less over and over again.

Perhaps the hardest thing in all this is figuring out when you need to keep working and when you need to give up and find a new vision. As a kid, I wanted to be a professional baseball player. No amount of magic and no amount of mundane effort was ever going to make that a reality—I simply don't have the necessary athletic ability. I had to give that up. But I figured out I could be a pretty good engineer, and that's worked out well... and I was able to play low-level amateur softball for about ten years.

You will fail. Progressive magic recognizes failures quickly so practitioners don't prolong and repeat them.

REVIEW, REVISE, AND REPEAT

If you keep opening the oven to check on your cake, it will fall. Likewise, constantly checking the progress of your magic is a good way to insure it will fail. Give it time to work, and especially give it time to work in ways you may not have considered. But at some point, stop and take stock of how things are going. Is your magic working? Are you making progress toward your vision? Or do you need to try something different?

More importantly, is your vision still what you want? Perhaps you're a little closer to your goal and now you can be a little more specific. Or perhaps the closer you get, the more you realize this isn't really what you want. A major change of direction can be costly (in time and energy, as well as financially) but the sooner you can change course, the less costly it will be, and the less likely you'll end up somewhere you really don't want to be. I wish I had realized that being a corporate executive wasn't what I wanted when I graduated from college, but better to realize it at age thirty-five than to never realize it at all.

If you need to adjust or change your vision, do. Then go back to working on two levels: keep your long-term vision in your mind but also find a specific target for your magical and mundane efforts. If it works, keep it up. If it doesn't, make changes as quickly as you can. Then review your progress again.

The Tao Te Ching says that "a journey of a thousand miles begins with a single step." It continues with a second step, then a third, then a fourth, and on and on and on. It will likely involve side tracks and wrong turns, but with mindfulness and perseverance, we will reach the destination we want to reach.

PROFESSIONAL MAGICIANS

When we're just starting out, whether with magic or with the religious experience of gods and spirits, any result is a good result. Even a weak result gives us first-hand evidence that this is real and that it's worth investing time and energy into learning how to do it effectively. Even a trivial result motivates us to dive deeper. But then we have to make that deep dive and start getting better. We have to study and draw on the experience of those who've gone before us. We have to practice, so we build our skills. We have to review our results, so we can be sure our magic is bringing what we expect it to bring. And we have to make adjustments, since we rarely get things perfect the first time.

Becoming skilled takes years but the total number of years you've been practicing isn't always relevant. I know people who've been doing the same thing year after year, always sticking to what they've always done, never challenging themselves to learn something new. And I know people who discovered Paganism, committed to study and practice, and within a year were ahead of people with a decade's worth of experience.

Practice doesn't make perfect, perfect practice makes perfect. When we work magic the right way consistently, we put ourselves on the path to becoming professional magicians.

Here I use "professional" not to mean someone who gets paid or does something full time. Rather, I'm using the term to refer to someone who's put the necessary work into learning their craft and is really good at it.

Every now and then I come across someone who calls themselves a natural witch. Like everything else in life, the capacity for magic isn't evenly distributed across the population. Magic comes easy for some and very hard for others. Natural witches will get better than average initial results. If they work at developing their craft, they can reach some truly amazing levels of magic. If they don't work at it, they'll soon be passed by the ordinary folks who are practicing more diligently.

The time to practice is before there is a need. For most of my Pagan life, I worked magic on an as-needed basis. If life was going well, I figured, why bother with magic? Ordinary actions are more reliable and are often easier; done right, magic is a lot of work. It's when ordinary actions aren't yielding satisfactory results or when the need is beyond the reach of ordinary actions that most of us turn to magic. And then we discover that our skills aren't up to the task, because we didn't practice (or didn't practice enough) during ordinary times.

Even in societies where magic was a part of everyday reality, ordinary people weren't magicians. They would pray and make offerings and pay attention to signs and omens. But if they needed serious magic, they went to the local witch or in some cases the local priest. They went to the professional magician.

So, either become a professional magician and get really good at it (in which case you should expect people to start coming to you for magical help) or support your local witch so they have the time and resources to dedicate to becoming really skilled at magic.

7

DIVINATION AND ORACLES

I'VE RECEIVED ONE CONSISTENT message from the beginning of my time as a Pagan: focus on the work at hand. I knew I needed to study, but study for what? Doesn't matter, just study. I knew I needed to practice, but practice for what? Doesn't matter, just practice. Even when it was clear I was on a long-term path, such as when I joined OBOD and started the Bardic lessons, all I could ever see was what was right in front of me. I knew I had to climb the next hill but had no idea what I'd find once I got to the top.

The message of focusing only on what was in front of me was necessary to break me of my fetish for grand plans. Now, if you're going to build a house, you need a full set of plans. But if you don't know how many people are going to live in the house or what they'll do in the house besides eat and sleep, you can't do a very good job of drawing plans. The best course is to maintain optionality: keep your options open as long as you can and remain open to new information and possibilities.

Given my natural inclination to focus on the future, it's no surprise that one of the first magical tools I bought was a deck of tarot cards. And given the emphasis of the messages I've received, it's also no surprise I had little success with them, partly because I needed some in-person instruction and a lot of practice, but more importantly because I was trying to use divination to find big goals and devise big plans. If I've learned anything about divination in the succeeding years, it's that divination doesn't do a very good job of telling you what you should do. Divination will show you where a given path or course of action is likely to take you, but it's up to you to figure out if that's a good thing or not.

When things are difficult, I tend to focus even more heavily on doing today's work today. That's something I have control over. I can't fix climate change or religious bigotry or the state legislature, but I can fix a chapter in my book or get today's blog post finished. I can do today's spiritual practice. There's always the danger of getting so tied up in things that are urgent but insignificant that we forget about things that are more important but perhaps more far off. Taking care of what you can do instead is far better for yourself and for the world at large than obsessing over what you can't do. At some point, however, focusing solely on the work at hand becomes self-limiting and can even become dangerous. When you keep your eyes so focused on the path in front of you, you'll miss the lion in the bushes off to the side.

The days when you could keep your head down, do your job, and everything would work out just fine are long gone ... if they even ever existed. The rate of change in the world continues on its exponential growth curve, not just with technology but with economics, politics, religion, and culture as well. Many of the changes in our modern world aren't for the good, at least for those who aren't already rich and powerful. Even if we're alert and aware, dealing with the world is getting harder and harder. It helps to know what's coming, which is where divination comes into play.

A NEED FOR DIVINATION

When we approach divination as more than a parlor game and fortune telling, it can be a powerful tool to help us navigate difficult and uncertain times. There are many forms: scrying, runes, bibliomancy, geomancy, and more. There's no evidence the ancient Celts used ogham runes for divination, but it hasn't stopped modern Druids from divining with them. My favorite method is tarot; the more I practice, the more I've learned to see messages in the imagery and not just quote back the standard interpretations. It's taken me a long time, though.

Divination can't "tell your future." Too many variables are involved and asking a vague question will give you a vague answer. Beyond that, however, divination can do three main things for us: tell us where we are going, show us what we aren't seeing, and allow us to ask questions of the divine or spirits.

Walk down any path and you'll eventually end up somewhere. Divination won't give you the coordinates of where that is, but it will tell you what things will look and feel like when you get there. Does that look and feel good to you? If so, keep going. If not, you should probably make some changes. I strongly believe the future is not fixed but at some point, accumulated choices start to look like destiny. Remember that any question about where you're going can never be answered with finality. You're going to keep moving throughout your life until you die … and then you'll move on to whatever comes after death. If the answer to "where am I going?" seems incomplete, it's because you're only seeing one part of a longer journey. The older we get and the more difficult navigating the world becomes, the harder it gets to extract ourselves from bad situations to move toward what we really want and need. Divination will help you make course corrections sooner and avoid major backtracking.

While not a very good map, divination is an excellent set of head-lights. It won't tell you how long something will take (or at least, it won't tell me; I have zero luck with divining time frames) but it will show you the major obstacles you'll encounter on your way. Any warnings are likely to be less specific than you'd like—your job is to be on the lookout for something that fits the general description. It is also your job to take actions that are both appropriate and realistic. If a reading says you're going to get run over by a beer truck, you probably can't stop the truck from going out of control. You can, however, be somewhere else when that happens or steer out of its path because you saw it coming a split second earlier than you would have otherwise. There are a lot of danger-ous things going on in our world today; many are going on in secret. The mainstream media can only tell you what it sees, and it will only tell you what it thinks will grab your attention. Divination can tell you what things are coming that the media either can't see or won't tell you.

Divination allows you to ask questions of the gods and spirits. While there is certainly a psychological aspect to divination (particularly when you're reading for yourself) the word itself points us toward its source: divination comes from the divine. There is no substitute for ecstatic, mystical, and worshipful experiences of the gods. But what about those times when you just need an answer? "Is this sacrifice acceptable?" "Is this candidate ready to be your priestess?" "Is this message really what you want me to tell this person?"

As Pagans and polytheists trying to reimagine old religions for new times (or in some cases develop entirely new religions) and living good lives in the process, it's necessary for us to stay focused on the tasks at hand. That said, we also need to make sure we know where our paths will take us and what obstacles or opportunities we might be overlook-ing. And yes, sometimes we need an answer from the gods.

Like everything else in life, divination comes easier to some than to others, but almost anyone can do it with proper instruction and lots of practice. If it's just not your thing or you aren't comfortable with it yet, there are plenty of good diviners in our wider communities. As life becomes tougher, it helps to be forewarned.

A LEGACY OF ORACLES AND SEERS

When I start to describe the particular version of polytheism I practice, one of the adjectives I include is "oracular." At its most basic level, this means that the gods speak to us here and now. This is an ancient practice that was mostly abandoned by the Western world as of the Christian era. Reviving it reclaims a sacred tradition and emphasizes the presence of the gods in our world.

Most people have at least heard of the Pythia, the oracle of Apollo at Delphi. The origins of this oracle are not known, but it was established by the eighth century BCE and continued into the fourth century CE. A priestess would sit on a high stool, gaze into a shallow dish of water, and answer questions brought by everyone from kings to common people (larger offerings to the temple got you a better place in line—some things never change). Her proclamations were said to be infallible, though they were often vague and subject to interpretation by the attendant priests.

Modern scholars speculate that the Pythia's visions were caused by her inhaling the vapors seeping up through a crack in the rocks, or perhaps by some other naturally occurring chemical in the smoke from incense and offerings. Whatever the method, an altered state of consciousness was and often is necessary to hear messages from the gods.

The Greeks placed oracles in a different category from seers and diviners. These were the priests and priestesses who would read omens in nature, in the entrails of sacrifices, or using various divinatory systems. While I know of no ancient Druid oracles (which doesn't mean they didn't have them, considering how little we know about the ancient Druids), the Druids were the seers and diviners of the Celtic world. The

Ovate grade in the contemporary Order of Bards, Ovates and Druids is inspired by these seers.

I generally group divination together with direct messages from the gods when I speak of an oracular tradition, but the Greeks were right that they're not the same things. Both methods use an intermediary between us and the gods. In the case of divination, that intermediary is something objective: a cloud formation, a bird's cry, a particular arrangement of tarot cards. We can debate the proper interpretation but the sign itself exists independently of our thoughts about it. In the case of an oracle, the intermediary is another human. Unlike a tarot spread where everyone can see the same cards, we have no way to know for sure just who—or what—the oracle is seeing and hearing, or how accurately information is being relayed to us.

We know (many from personal experience) that becoming a skilled tarot reader requires years of training, study, and practice. Likewise, becoming a competent oracle also requires years of work. And because pure oracular work was mostly a lost art for centuries, finding a teacher is extremely difficult. We are in the earliest stages of reviving and rebuilding it.

A few people have a strong natural talent for hearing the gods. This sounds nice, but it can also be overwhelming and inconvenient. And then there's the matter of what the gods actually say when they choose to speak directly to us. It's rarely to tell us everything's going to be okay. More often the message goes, "Here's what I want you to do for me" even though we may have no idea how to do what they're asking.

An oracular tradition is a living tradition because the gods are always speaking to us. This fact makes it difficult to establish orthodoxy, so it's no surprise that religions which insist on orthodoxy have devalued or repressed oracular and divinatory practices, even when such communication comes directly from their god. The Catholic church teaches that public revelation ended with the apostles. Private revelation is acknowledged but has no authority for anyone other than the person who received it, and it can never be added to official church teachings no matter how widespread it becomes or how accurate and helpful it proves to be.

The Evangelical Protestant tradition in which I grew up went even further than that, claiming that after the ascension of Jesus, their god spoke only through the Bible and never through people. Claims of private revelation weren't just non-authoritative, they were "counterfeits of the devil." When the foundation of your religion is *sola scriptura*, there is no room for any other voice … even the voice of your god.

The danger that an oracle or a diviner will mistake their own voice for the voice of a god is real. I have had direct communications from gods and spirits that I had zero doubts were authentic. I've had others where I wasn't so sure; this is not an exact science. If a stranger calls out to me from across a crowded hotel lobby, I may not even hear them, much less recognize them. But if a close friend calls me—even if I haven't seen them face to face in a year or more—I'll recognize their voice and hear their words even over the background noise of a busy hotel lobby. If you've worked with a particular deity or ancestor or spirit for a long time, you are much more likely to recognize their voice in an oracular setting. Even with that, there are times when I get a message and am still unsure if it's them or if it's me. In those cases, I usually do a brief divination (such as a three-card tarot spread) and ask, "Is this really what you want me to do?"

It helps to have a tradition and a group in which to study and work, someone who can say, "In our experience, these signs usually mean this and not that." It helps to have someone who knows you well enough to say, "That wasn't you speaking in the circle tonight." And it *really* helps to have someone who can say, "You know, that doesn't sound quite right. Let me do my own oracular work and see if I can verify it." Verification is particularly important when you're dealing with beings who aren't gods because while the gods are virtuous, non-divine spirits will lie. And while the Fair Folk either can't or won't lie, they will tell the truth in confusing ways. Our ancestors usually mean well but just because they're spirits doesn't mean they know everything or that they're free from the prejudices and lack of good judgement they exhibited when they were alive. Even if you're 100 percent sure a message isn't coming from inside your own head, don't assume it has to be good and true and helpful.

We are wise, I think, to treat oracular pronouncements with a bit of skepticism. The concept of UPG (unverified personal gnosis, see the next section) encourages us to respect others when they tell us they have a message from the gods, and it encourages seers and oracles to temper their expectations of how others will receive their messages. But when multiple people in the same or even different traditions are hearing the same thing, we can have more confidence in the accuracy of the messages. Over time, we learn that the messages some people relay are usually pretty close to right, so we trust their work more than the work of others.

Over longer periods, the messages we receive through oracles and seers become incorporated into our traditions, helping them to grow in depth and effectiveness.

Oracles and seers are not a mandatory feature of polytheism. You can give religious regard to many real gods and still believe they don't speak directly to us. Without an oracular tradition, however, Pagan and polytheist religions will become stagnant. Or worse, those practices will be swayed by the whims of popular culture and the mainstream society.

Oracles and seers are an important part of the polytheism I practice. They are a sacred tradition worth restoring and a reminder of the presence of the gods in our world.

CONTINUOUS UPG: THE "GOD-PHONE"

Mystical experiences happen more frequently than we realize. Some are brief moments of wonder and awe. Others are longer and deeper. While we may not be able to explain them to the satisfaction of skeptics, we are quite sure they carry a specific meaning. We call these experiences unverified personal gnosis, or UPG. "Gnosis" means knowing. "Personal" means it's for us. "Unverified" means we can't prove it means what we think it means with any degree of certainty. The concept of UPG allows us to accept our mystical experience at the value that seems right to us without insisting that other people who didn't share in that experience treat us as some kind of authority. That's a responsibility most of us don't want.

These experiences come on their own timetable. Some people desperately want them but never have them. Some seem to have them only at inconvenient times, and a few have them virtually non-stop. Perhaps they have a strong natural talent for hearing the gods, or perhaps a particular god or spirit has a very strong connection with them. They call these experiences the "god-phone" where all they have to do is pick up the line and let the information flow. Some can't shut it off, describing it as being on a speaker phone that can't be hung up. In this case, these people are caught in a continuous flow of UPG. Does that sound like schizophrenia? It might be, but not necessarily. According to the Mental Health Foundation, as much as 28 percent of the general population hears voices either audibly or in their heads. Only about a quarter of those (7 percent of the total population) also have a psychotic disorder. As with most medical institutions, the Mental Health Foundation attempts to explain these voices in strictly nontheistic terms; in many cases, this is correct. But there are reports of gods and spirits speaking to people throughout history, and there is no reason to assume that the phenomenon no longer happens just because we're all educated and sophisticated products of Western culture. There is a need for religious awareness and sensitivity on the part of mental health professionals; it should be a given but often isn't.

I do not personally have a god-phone, but as my devotional practice has deepened over the years, the frequency of my communication with the gods has also increased. The deities with whom I have formal relationships are never far away. That doesn't mean they'll always answer if I call. Neither does it mean their messages (intended for me or to relay to others) are always crystal clear. Sometimes they are and sometimes they aren't… and sometimes they are but I wish they weren't, because they're hard. In those cases, I do my best to confirm the UPG with divination.

Continuous UPG is a sacred obligation. The people who brag about having a god-phone are the ones I tend to avoid. I hear too much trivial information from them and too much that builds them up as self-appointed authorities. If something sounds unbelievable, remember that you are under no obligation to believe it. That's the "personal" part of UPG—it's only authoritative for the person who received it. However, if information comes from a person you generally consider reliable, is in alignment with what is known about a particular god or spirit, and especially if your own intuition tells you there's something to it, you may want to pay attention.

8

ECSTATIC PRACTICE

Mystical experiences are found in every religion: instances of mystery and wonder, beauty and power that overwhelms us, often spontaneous in nature. They are first hand experiences of spiritual beings and of knowing things we had no way of knowing. Many are ineffable—impossible to describe in words.

For the most part, these experiences are not harmful but can be dangerous. They can turn your life upside down, show you life as it really is, and cause you to reevaluate your priorities. Many people who have mystical experiences rationalize them away, some because their worldview says experiences like this are fake and some because they don't want to deal with the implications.

Mystical experiences are very real, however. It's important to talk about them and support each other: together we can start building a new consensus reality that has room for these most meaningful and powerful religious, spiritual, and magical experiences.

Mystical experiences happen in their own time. We can invite gods and ancestors to speak to us, but they are sovereign beings just as we are. They may choose to come or not. Even beings who are traditionally summoned (i.e., demons) don't always show up on demand. Natural forces can have great impact on us but are even more difficult to predict.

One of the simplest ways to promote a mystical experience is simply to stand outside under the full moon. That's easy, but the moon is only full three days of the month. If the sky is overcast during those three days, you won't be able to see it. It's still there and you can still do full moon magic, but experiences of mystery and wonder are less likely to occur without that beautiful bright light in the sky. On the other hand, if you never go outside at night, you're guaranteed to never see the full moon. All you can control are your actions; results come in their own time.

It helps to build a foundation of regular devotion. If you want gods and spirits to talk to you, start by talking to them. Create an altar, pray, meditate, and make offerings. Read, study, and talk with more experienced practitioners about what works and doesn't work for them. Above all, be consistent. Lots of people call on gods when they're in trouble or when they're curious—far fewer demonstrate the consistent dedication that shows they're looking for a relationship and not a parlor trick.

Do the prep work. We cannot command mystical experiences, but we can facilitate them, making them more likely to occur. Put yourself in the right frame of mind: grounding and centering will help you let go of the stress of ordinary life, if only for a short time. Light candles and incense. Wear your magical jewelry. Do whatever preparatory ritual you do: cast a circle, call the spirits of the directions and elements, invoke the land, sky, and sea. Find some good devotional readings and read them out loud, even if you're the only one present... or *especially* if you're the only one present. Make offerings. Put some effort into researching traditional offerings or offerings that contemporary practitioners have found to be favorably received.

Does this preparatory work increase the odds a spiritual being will speak to you or does it increase the odds you'll hear them if they do speak? A little of both, I think. All I know is that it helps.

The gods can speak to you anywhere, but nature spirits are far more likely to speak to you in the wild because that's where they are. Experiences of wonder and awe in nature can happen in the woods or desert or oceanside, but they're not going to happen in your living room. There is magic in wild places; if you want to have a mystical experience, visiting wild places greatly increases your chances.

There is nothing like spending time in true wilderness. Visiting accessible natural places is the next best thing: parks and rural areas work well, and even your back yard will do. Maybe you can only visit true wilderness once a year, but you can visit a local park once a week or so and can spend time in your backyard every night. If you don't have a backyard, put some plants in your kitchen window. Making use of what you have is far more effective than doing nothing because you don't have access to the ideal environment.

Spontaneous mystical experiences can happen at any time of the day —one of my strongest was in the middle of the afternoon. If you're trying to encourage one, it helps to work with as little light as possible both indoors or outdoors. Darkness blocks out distractions and focuses our concentration on our immediate surroundings. And really, most of us associate magic and mystery with the dark. That's one more thing to put us in the right frame of mind.

Have patience and be persistent. You can do all these things with perfect intention and perfect execution and still get nothing. Mystical experiences cannot be commanded. Sitting outside for fifteen minutes didn't produce anything? Next time try thirty minutes. Or two hours.

Or from dusk till dawn. Or try an hour every night for a month. Does that sound excessive? It may very well be, but that doesn't mean it's wrong. Spiritual experiences happen on their own timetable. Gods and spirits speak to us when they choose, but I have found that persistence will often get their attention when hit-or-miss practice will not.

Some practitioners use entheogens—chemicals (mostly from plants) that produce a change in consciousness that make a mystical experience more likely. Most of them are illegal, and with good reason: the wrong dosage can kill you, and you'll hurt a lot while you're dying. But people have used herbs, mushrooms, and other psychoactive substances in rituals for thousands of years; when used properly, they work. If you feel this is for you, find an experienced practitioner to guide you through it (note that this will probably mean you'll have to leave the country to do it.)

The only entheogen I've ever used is alcohol. I won't touch it before a public ritual, but I've found it to be helpful in certain private rituals. For me, the "goldilocks zone" is when I'm legal to drive *but* not safe to drive. At this stage, I'm still able to focus on what I'm doing but my filters are lower: I'm more open to unusual inputs and experiences and am less likely to judge them while they're happening.

Ecstatic experiences can be addictive, so handle them with reverence. There is nothing that can compare to a mystical or ecstatic experience, whether it's a message from a god or the vision of a spirit or the loss of self and sense of unity that comes with natural experiences of wonder and awe. When you have one, you'll want to have another and another and another. Mystical experiences aren't cookies—they don't happen for your enjoyment. Furthermore, sometimes they aren't enjoyable at all: they can sometimes be painful, difficult, or sometimes they call us to do something that is painful and hard. Most importantly, they're sacred. And because they're sacred they must be handled with reverence, appreciation that they have a sacred source and purpose that connects you to something bigger than yourself. Show these experiences the respect they deserve.

Mystical experiences take many forms but are found across every culture, including our mainstream culture. Most people ignore them or rationalize them away, but for those of us who understand and appreciate them, they can be the deepest, most meaningful experiences in our lives. We cannot control or command them, but through deep practice we can make experiences like these more likely in our lives.

TRAVEL IS GOOD FOR THE SOUL, INCLUDING TRAVEL BEYOND THE VEIL

Travel is one of the most educational and life-expanding activities you can do. It gets you out of your comfort zone. Travel—especially international travel—puts you in new and different situations. Sometimes that's fun and sometimes it's frustrating, like when flights get canceled and luggage gets lost. But even in these situations you figure things out, do what you need to do, and learn and grow in the process.

Travel lets you experience things firsthand. I've read and watched plenty on Islam, but being in a Muslim country gave me an understanding I couldn't get any other way. A bus ride into the Yukon showed me what wilderness really means, and exploring Orkney was a pilgrimage in every sense of the term.

If you don't have the resources for big trips, I strongly encourage you to take smaller, less expensive trips. Go somewhere while you still can. Go before your health declines and family obligations make it impossible to get away. Go before development, war, or climate change alter the places you want to see beyond recognition. Just go.

The benefits of mundane travel also apply to otherworldly travel.

Some people (including some theistic and magical Pagans) view otherworldly travel as an escape. "It's not 'real,'" they say. Even if they believe it's possible, they don't consider otherworldy travel a good use of their time, saying that it's "too out there" (and in some cases, "too 'New Age'") for serious Pagans to put much stock in it. Never mind the fact that most people who have mystical and otherworldly experiences describe them as the most real things they've ever known.

I have misgivings about the traditional upper world-middle world-lower world model of the cosmos, but there is value in journeying to the upper and lower worlds, whatever they may be. We can see how things are in an idealized state and then work to manifest them here in the middle world. We can see things that are important but hidden and then bring them out into the open, where we can deal with them more effectively. We can learn the wisdom of the depths.

We can journey backward (and perhaps forward) in time to recover lost information, meet ancestors whose names we will otherwise never know, and learn more about ourselves and our origins. Can we change the past while we're there? I tend to think not, but maybe it's possible.

The Otherworld is home to gods and ancestors as well as other spiritual beings. Sometimes they come here, but we can go visit them in their homes other times. Should you wish to visit, great caution and diplomacy are advised ... but there is great value in visiting them.

Our journeys at Samhain are perhaps the most beneficial. We visit with our ancestors and peer into the Otherworld, and the unknown becomes a little more known. Then when death comes as eventually it does for everyone, we will not be afraid because we will remember our journeys and we will have at least some idea where we're going and what it's going to be like when we get there.

Once again for emphasis: Otherworldly travel is not a cruise—it's not first-class travel planned by a competent agent. It's not even budget air travel and youth hostels. Otherworldly travel is an American on foot in an Asian country without any knowledge of the native language, no cellular service, an out-of-date map, and a wallet that has plenty of money but in all the wrong currencies. In other words, it's doable but quite the challenge, and it really helps to have an experienced traveler along with you, particularly the first couple of times.

Read the stories of our ancestors—the dangers are real. It's one thing when otherworldly beings come into our world, but it's quite another when we venture into their territory. Be polite, gracious, scrupulously honest, and above all pay attention. As with so much else beyond the basics of Paganism, this isn't for everyone. Here is required a certain curiosity, determination, and to be perfectly honest, a certain arrogance. What makes you think you can go where the living aren't intended to go and make it back in one piece? Not everyone who tries can do it, and not everyone who does it comes back unharmed … but some do. We contemplate what's out there, how we can get there, and what we'll encounter when we're there. And then we go.

PARTING THE MISTS:
AN INTRODUCTION TO JOURNEYING

I hate to start with a disclaimer, but this needs to be said: journeying is best learned face-to-face. It is not risk-free; you can do it wrong and can end up in some places you don't want to be with some persons who aren't particularly nice. The topic is also subject to derision and ridicule by skeptics, which makes it that much more difficult for those attempting to learn it. But it's a good and helpful practice, and face-to-face teachers can be hard to find, so I'm including it in this book.

As with the rest of my practices, my approach to journeying is built on the foundational assumptions of animism, polytheism, and the primacy of religious experiences. A lot of people approach journeying from a psychological viewpoint. There can be value in that approach but too often it's an excuse to cling to materialist assumptions. And in any case, I'm a Druid and a priest, not a psychologist.

Journeying is the first-hand experience of other times, other places, and other realms. The description is rather vague but it's the best I've got. It's similar to dreaming, remote viewing, and out of body experiences but is not any of those things. It can be directed (as in a guided meditation) but cannot be controlled. What you experience depends on where you actually go and on your interactions with the persons you encounter. For example, you can journey to meet an ancestor but cannot compel that ancestor to come to you; if they do come, you cannot control what they say and do.

Journeying isn't Otherworldly tourism—it's not something you do just to see what's over there. It's something you do for a purpose: to form and strengthen relationships with spiritual beings, find knowledge you can't get otherwise, and learn something you need to learn so you can do something you need to do. If we lived in a magical and animistic society, we would grow up seeing examples of journeying and learn how to do it ourselves. We don't, so the skills don't come easily to most of us—we have to work at it.

Reading fiction is perhaps the most useful exercise to prepare you for journeying. Any fiction will do, it doesn't have to be fantasy or magically-oriented. In some ways it's better if it isn't to avoid setting unreasonable expectations. Reading fiction is to journeying as weight lifting is to playing football—it improves fitness for the primary activity. Fiction trains the mind to see with inner eyes.

Practicing visualization is another big help. See an apple in your mind's eye. See yourself pick it up, see its colors and feel its skin. In your mind, take a bite: experience the tastes on your tongue and the textures in your mouth. Set it back down and see it sitting there with a bite taken out of it. Do this and similar exercises until you're comfortable with the process.

A significant minority of people (I've heard estimates from 10 to 25 percent) simply can't visualize. They can't "see" with their mind but can hear or touch or smell. If that's you, find another method that works for you: imagine sounds or touch.

Remember that changing consciousness is a means, not the end goal. I do not know if it is impossible to journey into the Otherworld in an ordinary state of consciousness or if it is just extremely difficult. I know I need a setting free of distractions. Setting an Otherworldly atmosphere helps, such as a darkened room with candles or outdoors at night around a fire. Learning to meditate helps, as it teaches you to focus on one thing, not the hundreds of inputs your mind receives at any given moment. Drumming and dancing are traditional ways of changing consciousness. If you don't have anybody to drum for you, there are recordings available. I have an app on my phone called "Shaman Magic" that's very good for this.

When practitioners discuss journeying, they often speak of parting the mists or the veil, jumping the hedge, crossing the bridge … there are many metaphors for moving from this world into the Otherworld.

I want to be very clear what I mean when I call this a metaphor; I do not mean it's not real or that it doesn't exist outside your head. What actually happens is unclear and uncertain. I think we're all doing the same thing but are seeing it differently. I might be wrong, however—there may be multiple ways of accessing the Otherworld. Again, understanding this intellectually is far less important than experiencing it and learning from it.

After relaxing, grounding, and centering, I project myself into an idyllic countryside. From there it's a short walk to a sacred tree or a forest clearing, to a cave or a mountain, or to wherever I need to go to see and do whatever it is I need to see and do.

What do you do when you're there? Again, this isn't tourism. On one of my early journeys I went into a great library where I was promptly told, "You can browse when you're dead. Get to work or go back where you came from."

The main thing I do on these journeys is listen. Whether I'm encountering gods, ancestors, other spiritual beings, or simply the otherworldly environment, I want to take in as much of it as I can. However long I'm there (and sometimes it feels like days even though it isn't) it's never long enough. If I have questions, I'll ask them, even though I almost never get a straightforward answer; more often I'm called to receive a message or an instruction. Most times it's for me but sometimes I'm to relay it to someone else.

It helps to have allies: gods and ancestors who will point you in the right direction and give you their protection. Remember that they're allies, not servants. Treat them with all due honor and respect. Also remember that gods are virtuous, but spirits often lie. The fae either can't or won't lie but will spin the truth so fast you'll think up is down. Trust has to be built both ways. You need to learn who you can trust to tell you the honest and helpful truth, and the various Otherworldly persons need to learn that they can trust you to use what they give you in a virtuous manner. Assume nothing.

There are two problems in figuring out what's true and what's not. The first, as discussed above, is that some Otherworldly beings lie. And while gods won't lie, most are anything but clear and transparent. The second problem is that even though journeying isn't all in your head (when done correctly, anyway), it's all processed through your head. Separating Otherworldly messages from your own thoughts is challenging. Begin with some honest self-examination. If you know who and what you are, it's much easier to recognize when a thought is your own and when it's coming from someone else.

Is the message telling you something you want to hear or something you already know? It's probably your own thoughts seeping through. Is it telling you something you find challenging but deep down know is true? It's probably for real.

Is it consistent with the character of the person talking to you? Ancestors don't suddenly become paragons of virtue and fonts of wisdom just because they're dead. The Morrígan isn't likely to deliver messages of comfort, and Cernunnos isn't likely to tell you to buy stock in coal mining companies.

If you're not sure about what you hear, pull out your favorite divination tool. And if you're *still* not sure, consult a competent diviner who knows nothing about your situation. At the end of the day, you have to decide if what you heard or saw is true or not and if it is, how you should respond. If you need black and white certainty, journeying probably isn't for you.

Guided meditations are pretty safe, particularly if your guide knows what they're doing. Journeying is more difficult and more hazardous. The best way to learn it is with a face-to-face teacher. The second-best way is with an experienced partner who can watch over you and pull you back if you get into trouble and discuss your experiences after you're finished. But the fact is that many—perhaps most—people don't have access to face-to-face teachers. And while you sometimes may be able to find a minder, you're not likely to have one available when and where you need one every time. Most people are going to try it on their own.

Practice the techniques. Know the risks. Begin with prayers and offerings. Go in with your eyes wide open and make no assumptions. Treat everyone you meet with dignity and respect ... and caution. Watch and listen. Then come back and figure out what it all means.

I wish you safe travels and safe home.

EXERCISE: GUIDED MEDITATION

The best way to learn to journey is face-to-face with a teacher. The second-best way is through guided meditations. Here's a guided meditation to meet the goddess Brighid. You can read through the text as you go, although that's difficult. You can read it aloud and record it on your phone and then play it back as you meditate. I have a spoken version of this on my blog at http://www.patheos.com/blogs/johnbeckett /2015/01/imbolc-a-solitary-ritual.html and on YouTube at https:// youtu.be/eqrVDdDG2uI.

Get comfortable, close your eyes, and take a deep breath.

Take a second.

And a third.

In your mind's eye, see mists beginning to rise from the floor. See them rolling and growing, higher and higher, filling your circle. The mists are dense—you can't see anything around you anymore. But you can feel your surroundings, and the mists are warm and comforting.

Now the mists begin to fade, and you find yourself at the edge of a large open meadow.

It's a February day, but the sun is bright and warm, higher in the sky than it was a few weeks ago. Breathe the clean air, and feel the new life beginning to stir just below the surface.

A path leads across the meadow, and you move forward. Have you been here before? Look around—what do you see? Listen—what do you hear? Keep walking.

The path leads up a hill, and at the top of the hill is a single evergreen tree reaching high into the sky. Greet the tree. Smell its fragrance, touch its rough bark, feel its solidity.

You notice movement, and you turn and see a woman walking up the other side of the hill. She has thick red hair and is dressed in a majestic green gown, and she carries a small harp she plays both effortlessly and beautifully.

As you listen to the music, thoughts and feelings begin to swirl inside you. What is it you're called to create? What song must you sing, what poem must you write, what thing of beauty must you make? What is your great art?

Yes, that's it!

Thank the Lady Brighid for her inspiration.

Now the mists begin to rise again. The woman and the tree fade from view, and the sound of the harp grows ever more faint.

You feel yourself moving through space and time, and when the mists begin to fade, you find yourself in a small village.

It is night, and the sky is dark. It is cold, and though the wind is low you feel it pulling the heat from your body. Winter is still very much with us.

At the end of the street you see light flooding out from an open door. Begin walking toward this light.

You walk through the door into brightness and warmth. A hot fire burns in the hearth, and the tools of metalworking are neatly arranged. This is the forge of Brighid.

A woman stands in front of the fire, the same woman you saw on the hill. She is still dressed in green, but her fine gown has been traded for the rough clothes of a smith. Her thick red hair has been pulled back, and her sleeves are rolled up to reveal strong arms. She swings a hammer, shaping a piece of bronze against a heavy iron anvil.

The woman looks at you and smiles. You have a part to play here. Are you the hammer, the instrument of the will of this great Goddess? Are you the anvil, supporting the work of others? Or are you the metal, going into the forge to be refined and shaped and tested, transformed into something more?

Thank the Lady Brighid for her smithcraft.

Now the mists begin to rise again. The woman and her work fade from view, and the heat of the forge is lost in the cool of the mists.

Again you feel yourself moving through space and time, and when the mists begin to fade, you find yourself in a forest of mighty oaks.

It is twilight, just before dawn. Through the trees you can see an orange glow on the horizon. Morning is coming, but the night has been long.

A short way into the forest is a well, and you realize you're thirsty. Begin walking toward the well.

As you approach, you see a woman standing beside the well. This is the sacred well of Brighid, one of many.

Once again she wears green, but this time it is the simple robe of a healer. The soot and sweat of the forge are gone; she is spotlessly clean.

The woman draws water from the well, then dips a cup into the bucket. She hands it to you. You drink, and the water is cool and clear.

The water does more than quench your thirst. It refreshes your body. It restores your will. It renews your soul.

Thank the Lady Brighid for her healing.

Yet again the mists begin to rise. The woman and the well fade from view, and again you feel yourself moving through space and time. The mists fade a final time, and you find yourself back in this place and this time.

When you're ready, open your eyes. Be here now.

PART 3:

CHALLENGES

9

OVERCOMING ROADBLOCKS

SOMETIMES OUR PAGAN PRACTICE is a beautiful and joyful thing. Most times it's a meaningful thing, even though it's a lot of work. But other times our Pagan practice seems flat. Fatigue turns into frustration, frustration turns into panic, and panic turns into resignation. Meanwhile, the world keeps moving and the need for the work we're doing is as dire as it's ever been.

This isn't the dark night of the soul, when everything seems hopeless and you feel like giving up. This is the dry season, when you want to keep moving but it's hard and joyless. The vision of a better world and a deeper practice is obscured by smoke and haze. When you're hungry but nothing sounds good, when the joy of summer has turned into the monotony of oppressive heat. Pick your metaphor—this is the time when it's not fun to be a Pagan.

The dry season is not unique to Paganism, but as Pagans we have a unique approach to deal with it.

When I was much younger, I ran two marathons. One of the things the marathon teaches is that if you refuse to give in to fatigue, you can accomplish great things. Another lesson of the marathon is that when you exhaust your body's supply of glycogen, you do what's called "hitting the wall," where you just can't keep up your usual pace, no matter how badly you want to. It's one thing to struggle through the final miles when you know the finish line is near. It's another thing entirely to keep running when you're sick and tired and there's no end in sight.

If you're just tired, skipping the gym for another hour of sleep may be enough. But if you're sick, that's not enough. Sometimes you need a weekend on the couch. Most times I come home from my paying job with plenty of energy for my Pagan work, but if I'm sick, I don't. Not much gets done. So be it; sometimes you have to rest.

During a dry season, the gods often go silent. The Morrígan has no new assignments, Brighid is silent about what she wants me to write, and even the local land spirits seem strangely quiet … but they're not missing. I can still sense them in their usual places during my daily prayers and weekly devotions. They're just not talking to me.

Are they being quiet out of compassion? Or are they off doing their own things for their own reasons that have nothing to do with me? I don't know. But I am sure that their lack of communication (and lack of intervention) has nothing to do with the state of our connections. No relationship is "on" all the time, including our spiritual relationships. Even our closest family members sometimes have stuff to do that doesn't involve us. Don't mistake silence for abandonment.

Even if the gods are silent, maintain your daily spiritual practice. I have to be deathly ill to go a day without brushing my teeth or taking a shower. I have to be about as sick to skip all my daily prayers. Our core practices keep us connected to our spiritual allies and remind us of what's most important, even if practice doesn't feel particularly important at the moment. They're a trickle of water in the desert. Even if it hurts to be reminded of the times when they were full of wonder and awe, the bit of power they provide can be the difference between keeping going and dropping out. Maintain your daily spiritual practice.

I've always been good at multi-tasking. When one thing stalls out or hits a "wait and see" phase, I would move on to something else. Multi-tasking isn't really working on multiple things at once, it's moving quickly from one thing to another. And in dry seasons, capacity isn't what it was during the good times. Where normally I can keep three or four projects going, now I'm struggling to manage two. Or one. And so choices have to be made.

Everything may be important. Everything may be equally important. But everything can't be first. Something has to be set aside. Too many of us can't afford to take time off from our paying jobs even when we're sick. If you can, do it. Working sick isn't a good thing. If you have to set projects aside, do it. Better that they wait till you can give them the attention they need than to shortcut something sacred. If hard choices have to be made, make them. Everything can't be first.

Dry seasons are like Mercury retrograde—they come and go. They don't last forever. Colds eventually go away. Paying jobs ease up. Leaky roofs get fixed. The gods start speaking again and those amazing ecstatic experiences return. Sometimes that takes weeks. Sometimes it takes months. Sometimes it takes years. If your Pagan beliefs and practices were meaningful to you before, they will be meaningful again, if you stay with them.

Sometimes, though, you just have to be the Druid. Or be the Witch or be the Heathen or be whatever it is you are. Put on your robes, fire up your cauldron, and start brewing the Awen. Light the incense and pour the offerings. Draw sigils, light candles, and cast spells. Whatever it is you do, just do it. Even if it doesn't feel like it's getting you anywhere, just do it.

This is where Paganism stands in stark contrast to mainstream culture. For most people in the West (especially Protestant Christians) religion is about what you believe. For Pagans and polytheists and most people around the world, religion is about what you do. More importantly, it's about who you are.

If you're a Druid, then you're a Druid even in the dry seasons. If you're a Witch, then you're a Witch even when you don't feel very witchy. Be the Druid. Be the Witch. Be the Pagan.

Dry seasons happen to all of us sooner or later. The realities of life intrude on our plans, and so we deal with them, as we must. Accept reality, take care of yourself, do what must be done, and then be the Pagan you are.

WHEN YOU CAN'T EXPERIENCE THE GODS FOR YOURSELF

The unmediated, firsthand experience of a god is an awesome thing. It's inspiring and empowering, as you see for yourself just what could be if we had their perspective on life. It's also humbling to realize that no matter how strong and wise we may be, there are beings who are far stronger and wiser than us.

What do you do when you can't experience the gods for yourself? I'm not talking about nontheists; that's an honorable path, but I'm specifically addressing those who very much want this experience but can't seem to get there.

As far as I've seen, most people can experience the gods for themselves sooner or later. However, our mainstream culture presents several impediments to this experience. It's important to know that none of them are your fault.

For all the advances we've made toward religious pluralism over the past hundred years or so, Western culture is still heavily Christianity-dominant: it teaches that there is only one god who is primarily concerned with what you believe. It tells us to put our faith in ancient writings about other people's experiences and insists that asking for our own experience shows a lack of faith. Christianity is not monolithic; there are many good Christians who follow the teachings of Jesus instead of the human-made doctrines about Jesus, but it is these conservative and fundamentalist ideas that dominate our culture and impede a widely-accepted understanding of polytheist concepts.

Another part of our mainstream culture tells us that people who experience gods and spirits first-hand are primitive, backward, and superstitious. Much of this religious prejudice is intertwined with racism and classism—ways the mainstream tells itself it's superior to "those people" and pressures us to conform.

There are many more examples. We grow up with no context for the direct experience of many gods and think it's not possible. Saying, "I believe in the gods," no matter how sincerely, doesn't wipe out all these cultural influences. Overcoming them takes time and effort.

Start by setting realistic expectations. Most times the experience of a god is a subtle thing: it's feeling the presence of another, signs and omens, and knowing something you had no way of knowing. It's a thought in your head you're pretty sure didn't come from you. Know yourself so you can recognize what's you and what's not-you. Don't expect something out of a movie. Don't expect to see something with your physical eyes or hear with your physical ears. These things do happen but are very rare. Perhaps the most important expectation you can set is "experience now, interpret later." Once you start analyzing an experience, the pressure to rationalize it away will be immense. In the moment, just go with it.

Practice regular devotion. If you want the gods to talk to you, start by talking to them. Pray and make offerings. Read their stories and sing their songs. Read what we know about them from mainstream scholarship. Perhaps most importantly, meditate. If you want anyone—god or mortal—to speak to you, you have to be quiet long enough to listen for them and then *to* them. If we lived in a polytheist society, you'd learn this growing up. Since we don't, you have to learn it where and when you can. There aren't a lot of groups that do this kind of work, and some will say they do but aren't doing what I'm describing here. Finding a group that can help you facilitate the first-hand experience of a god can be very difficult. But if you can, do it.

Keep working. It took me five years from the time I got serious in my Pagan practice until I had an experience of a god that was so strong I couldn't rationalize it away. It was another three years before it happened again. After that, the experiences started getting stronger and more frequent. Contact from deities comes easier for some than for others, so it may not take you as long as it did for me. It could also take longer. Remember that we are dealing with real gods with agency— whether they speak to you or not is ultimately up to them. But don't give up just because contact doesn't happen right away.

There is no test for god-blindness. Given all the cultural obstacles we face in learning to experience the gods, how can we ever be completely sure the problem is with the individual? Based on the people who have approached me about this topic and what I've read of others' experiences (not just in contemporary Paganism) it seems likely that some people are god-blind. Most of us have no trouble distinguishing between red and green. But if you have color blindness, no amount of wanting and trying is going to help you see one or the other. But if you genuinely want to experience the gods and you just can't, there are some things you can do.

Abandon all fundamentalist and Calvinist ideas. Calvinism teaches that their god chooses some for salvation and others for damnation for reasons unknowable by humans. If that doesn't make sense to you, you're obviously not one of the elected, so have fun in hell. The Calvinist philosophy is bad theology from a Christian standpoint (much less from a Pagan one) but it's part of the mainstream culture that affects us all, whether we're Christian, Pagan, or atheist. Your ability or lack thereof to experience the gods first-hand is no reflection of your virtue, and it's certainly no indication of your position in the afterlife. Live an honorable, virtuous, and (where possible) heroic life. Take care of yourself, your family, and those entrusted to you. Treat others with dignity and respect. Leave the world a better place than you found it. The rest will take care of itself. More to the point, never let anyone (including yourself) tell you you're less of a Pagan or less of a polytheist because you can't or haven't experienced the gods first-hand.

Practice regular devotion. Read, pray, study, meditate, and make offerings. We do these things not so the gods will give us awesome experiences but because it is always good to honor the gods. The more we dwell on them, the more their values and virtues become our values and virtues, and that's a very good thing.

Support the Pagan and polytheist communities. Perhaps you can't experience the gods first-hand. But you can make it easier for someone who comes after you to experience them. Perhaps your calling is not in ecstatic devotion but in academic research. Perhaps it's in theology or philosophy. Perhaps it's in building organizations. There are many things that need to be done to build a healthy Pagan and polytheist society. The more we can accomplish, the more we can lessen the mainstream culture's impact on us, and the more people will be ready to experience the gods for themselves.

Mainly, keep working. I don't believe in miracles, but I do believe in magic. Magic doesn't make things happen—it improves the odds that they will happen. Perhaps you aren't god-blind but just need to be in the right setting. Magic can help put you in the right setting. Perhaps you just need to catch the attention of the right deity. Perhaps there's only one more thing holding you back, and once you get past it, you'll have a breakthrough.

Or perhaps not. There is no such thing as certainty in religious matters. But your value as a person and your authenticity as a polytheist are not dependent on your ability to have these experiences.

Honor the gods. Live virtuously. Leave your corner of the world a better place than you found it. The rest will take care of itself.

DO THE GODS TEST PEOPLE?

"The gods are testing you." I can't tell you how many times I've heard that statement. Though more frequently, I'm told "God" or "Goddess" or "the Universe" is testing me. I don't hear the testing claim from polytheists very often. Any time I've gone through a long difficult stage in my life, someone has told me it's a test I have to pass before I can move on to whatever comes next. Sometimes I'm told that whatever is wrong is going to stay wrong until I learn some great cosmic lesson.

Interestingly, I've never had someone who's going through a hard time smile and say, "It's OK, it's just a test. I just have to learn what they want me to learn and everything will be fine." If what someone else is experiencing is a test, it's just for them; I can convince myself it won't happen to me. I can also convince myself it's all for their own good and so I have no obligation to help them. How convenient.

We humans have a strong desire to find meaning in suffering. While suffering can be educational and transformative, it is never redemptive—mainly it just is. As the Facebook meme says, everything happens for a reason—sometimes the reason is that you're stupid and make bad decisions. I would substitute "stubborn" for "stupid," as very smart people occasionally do very dumb things, myself included. And really, a lot of suffering is simply bad luck. Life is far more random than we like to think.

The stories of our ancestors tell us of small tests, such as Odin disguising himself as a lowly traveler to test the hospitality of various people. They also tell of great ordeals, such as the Twelve Labors of Hercules. But "tests" and "lessons" that drag out for months and years? That's just ordinary life with ordinary suffering that must either be remedied or transcended. And yet…

On several occasions I've talked to someone who went through a long difficult period in their life and came out much better for it. They concluded that this was a test from the gods, and they passed. Is that correct? Were the gods or a god testing them? What they experienced—hardship, struggle, pain—is a matter of fact. That they learned something helpful is also a matter of fact. Whether a god or gods were involved is a matter of interpretation that's impossible to verify objectively. Maybe the gods really were testing them. The fact that we can't be sure they were doesn't mean we can be sure they weren't. The Christian god is not the only one who works in mysterious ways.

The period from mid-2009 through early 2011 could easily have been a test for me. My paying job got very stressful. I started my blog and struggled with it. I was finishing my OBOD coursework and had no idea what to do next. I kept up my public and private spiritual practices but with a few exceptions, they brought only momentary relief. I was in a bad place and couldn't see any way forward. I never prayed the very dangerous prayer, "I'll give anything if only you'll fix this!" but I made it clear I was open to pretty much any opportunity for growth and service. Meanwhile, in the back of my head I wondered if my "Pagan thing" was over and I needed to go do something else instead.

I stayed with my practice. In 2011, I started working with a spiritual director. That got me off my spiritual plateau and moving forward again. And the mundane stress returned to normal, manageable levels.

Was this a string of coincidences or a test that I passed? Honestly, I don't know. None of the deities I work with have ever said it was, either in UPG or in divination. And I don't believe "the universe" makes plans for individuals. But in retrospect it sure looks like a test.

There are several reasons why tests—as they're commonly experienced and described—can be a good thing. Tests can confirm your commitment to the gods. My experience with the gods (or at least the handful I'm familiar with) has been very straightforward. They ask people they think can help them to do the things they want done. Show you can handle yourself and they'll keep giving you more. Tell them no and they'll move on to someone else. Tell them yes but don't keep your word and things will get unpleasant. But I've never been told, "First, prove you're worthy." On the other hand, it's been helpful to prove my commitment to the gods to myself. I know they're important to me and will continue to be important to me, so I can make long-term plans based on that commitment and be confident I'm not going to regret it five years down the road.

Tests can remind you of your true priorities. I began my professional career with the idea that I'd become a corporate executive. When I got a taste of what all that requires (short answer: a 24/7 obsession with your job) I figured out that wasn't my true calling. Lots of people want to be Pagan priests, and a lot fewer want to do all the hard and unglamorous work that being a priest entails. Even fewer want to do it day after day, season after season, year after year. And that's OK—our Pagan and polytheist religions need to have a place for people at all levels of interest and commitment. But if the reality of priestly work isn't something you want to do, you're better off realizing that sooner than later.

Tests can clear the deck for something new to come in. Feeling overwhelmed? Perhaps you need to cut back from five or six major commitments to one or two. Feeling drained? Maybe you need to remove some unhealthy people from your life so you'll have the energy you need for your next project.

Tests can force you to learn new skills you'll need further down the road. Necessity is the mother of invention. It's also the mother of learning. The need to lead rituals forced me to learn public speaking. The need to get spiritual direction helped me learn how to provide spiritual direction. The need to keep writing helped me learn to be a better writer. As science fiction writer Ray Bradbury said, "Everyone's first million words are crap"—the sooner you can get through those million words of crap, the sooner you can start writing good stuff (go read some of my blog posts from 2008 if you don't believe me).

Perhaps the greatest skill these tests teach is perseverance, the willingness and ability to keep going even when things get difficult... because sooner or later, things always get difficult. In your search to understand a painful time in your life, you may come to the conclusion that this is a test that if you can just get through (or over, or under, or around), things may not be wonderful but will be better. You may realize you have family obligations that prevent you from doing everything you want to do but you can still study and learn and be ready when your obligations are less constricting. You may come to some other positive interpretation that helps you get through a difficult time (a good thing), but you cannot jump to this conclusion for someone else. It's their life, so they have to find their own interpretation. Even if they're your closest friend—especially if they aren't—you don't know all the details of their situation. Telling someone that the divine beings they love and trust are doing this to them for reasons unknown is not going to be helpful.

If someone else comes to you, simply listen. Don't listen in order to offer advice unless they ask for it. Some people get mad when you offer unsolicited advice. I don't object to it, but I very rarely pay much attention to it. Instead, listen to hear how you can help. Most people won't ask for help, even if you say, "Just let me know if I can do anything," even if you mean it. If in doubt, the old Southern tradition of coming over and bringing food is still a good one.

So, do the gods test people? I still don't know. We often look for meaning where none exists. Some suffering is random, some is due to other people behaving badly, and some is our own damn fault. Yet I cannot deny that I've been through long difficult periods in my life where I came through better than I was before. There very well may have been a divine purpose behind it or some of it. No experience is a total loss, if we can learn from it.

DOUBT AND DEDICATION

Some forms of Christianity teach that doubt is a terrible sin. I occasionally hear atheists say that if you can't be absolutely sure about something—if you have any doubts at all—you should reject it. On the other hand, the first Unitarian Universalist sermon I ever heard was titled "Cherish Your Doubts"—it celebrated doubt as a way to keep us honest.

The only person with no doubts is a fool. Perhaps we can be absolutely certain about basic science and mathematics, although the progression of knowledge and theories in physics is a reminder to always remain open to new evidence and new ideas. In the realms of religion and philosophy, certainty is impossible.

In *The Path of Paganism*, I advised beginners to "practice deeply but hold loosely," or keep an open mind and be ready to change your beliefs if they discover they're wrong or if they find something better. But while you hold those beliefs, treat them as though they're absolutely true and explore them as deeply as you can. This is a very practical and useful approach, especially for beginners. If we follow it, we will find ourselves discarding erroneous beliefs and rededicating ourselves to helpful ones.

But the doubts never completely go away, especially in times of trouble. How can they? Our mainstream culture demands absolute proof, and we have none to offer. And no one else has absolute proof, despite the fact that some religions claim to have it. We may begin to wonder, "Am I wasting my time with this?" and "Maybe the atheists are right." There is no sin in doubt and there are no questions that cannot be asked. But it is not our beliefs that make us Pagan, it is our actions. If pouring offerings to your patron deity has been meaningful in good times, keep pouring offerings through the bad times. If saluting the rising sun has been helpful during good times, keep saluting it during the bad times. Keep doing the things that make you Pagan.

Most importantly, maintain your Pagan relationships. This means your local human relationships, as well as your online relationships with co-religionists across the world. It also means your relationships with the land where you live, the spirits who share the land with you, and your ancestors whose lines you continue and honor just by living. Good religion is about what you do, and it's also about who you are—where you belong. Maintain your relationships in good times and in bad.

If your doubts remain troubling, explore them. Ignoring them just allows them to fester under the surface and sets you up for more serious problems later on. Is there a problem with history? Scholarship gets better all the time—look for the most recent research. Is there an ethical problem? What are the virtues relevant to the situation, and how can you best exemplify them? Is it a problem of foundational assumptions? Re-read chapter 2, and make sure you aren't giving materialist assumptions more credibility than they deserve.

Unlike the UU minister who preached on cherishing doubts, I don't see them as entirely a good thing. I've found I get more done if I act as though I had certainty even when I can't be completely sure. But doubts are inevitable and can keep our "working certainty" from turning into arrogance. The good news is that we can work through our doubts, refine our beliefs and practices, and come out of challenging times stronger than we began.

10

LIVING WITH GODS
AND SPIRITS

OUR MANY POLYTHEIST RELIGIONS concern themselves with many different things, but near the top of almost every list is forming and maintaining relationships. We form relationships with our communities, with our ancestors, with the land and the spirits of the land, and with our gods.

These sacred relationships can take many forms. Some polytheists spend a lifetime honoring the gods and doing their work in this world and never go beyond that. Some experience the presence of the gods in ritual. Some speak with gods in dreams, meditation, and divination. Some experience ecstatic communion with a deity, feel their presence within themselves, and allow the deity to speak through them.

The intimate, ecstatic, personal presence of a deity can be an amazing experience, but they aren't the only way to be a Pagan. And sometimes this kind of presence brings us things we aren't expecting and or prepared for.

PRIESTHOOD, AND SACRED CALLINGS THAT AREN'T PRIESTHOOD

Priesthood is a specific set of duties and commitments that often looks very different from what Catholic priests and Protestant ministers do. There are many forms of service; priesthood is only one.

Priesthood is both a role and a relationship. A priest is a servant of a god or gods, but not all who serve the gods are priests. A priest has a clear relationship with a deity or deities, but having a patron deity does not make you a priest. That relationship is generally a formal one with oaths and covenants and sometimes with ordinations or initiations, but I mark the beginning of my priesthood from the time I was called, not from the time I swore oaths.

If you want to draw a clear line between priestly and non-priestly work, focus on the relationship, not on the role. My work with and for Cernunnos is virtually indistinguishable from my work with and for the Morrígan. But while my oath to Cernunnos is the oath of a priest, my oath to the Morrígan is not. I am not her priest, and I will never be her priest. And I'm perfectly fine with that.

I've had several people say the title of priest has to be conferred on you, either by your tradition or by a particular god—it's not something you can claim for yourself. I think that's a good way to look at it. Still, some activities are generally considered priestly work, while other activities are generally considered non-priestly even though priests may perform them.

Priests serve the gods. A Methodist minister once told me, "I serve God by serving people." For ancient polytheists, especially those in the Mediterranean area, such a statement could be reversed. They served people by serving the gods. The priests made offerings and sacrifices, cared for the temples and shrines, and performed sacred rituals. By doing what must be done, they insured the blessings of the gods on their people. Why the gods need or want rituals and sacrifices is a good question (is it for them? is it for us? both? something else?) but both ancient and modern polytheisms make it clear—there are things the gods want from us.

Devotion is not only a priestly activity. I would argue it is virtually a requirement to consider yourself a polytheist. But it is an activity where a priest should be an expert as a result of both study and training as well as extensive practice.

Priests are ritual leaders, be they daily rituals, seasonal rituals, or rituals for special occasions. Some traditions require that some rituals only be performed by priests, but for the most part, anyone can lead a Samhain ritual. What makes a priest different is their expertise in these ritual from study, training, and extensive practice.

Priests are officiants who oversee weddings, funerals, initiations, and other rites of passage. Some of the tasks in this role come from the Christian mainstream, which expects a priest or minister to officiate. Our ancient ancestors didn't always feel this same need; some rites were family affairs while others were civic activities. Nevertheless, priests are expected to be able to perform officiant-related tasks.

Priests are oracles, voices of the gods that relay messages through signs and omens, divination tools and methods, and direct communication. The validity of an oracle's message is up to those who hear it. Good discernment is always required but ignore the proper warnings of an oracle at your peril. In ancient times, being an oracle was its own role, sometimes served or assisted by priests. Perhaps someday we'll have enough resources to support full-time oracles once again.

Priests are counselors. This is another holdover from contemporary Christianity. In ancient times, if you needed counsel you sought out a philosopher or a sage. But most Pagans and polytheists expect our priests to have the same skills as Christian priests and ministers, even though few of us have formal training. I'm happy to provide religious counseling, but if someone needs a mental health professional I have to step aside.

None of these activities are restricted to priests and doing them does not make you a priest. But they're things many priests do or are expected to be able to do. There are other activities that while priests may do them, are usually done by laity.

Community service and political activism aren't priestly work. I've seen several surveys describing how many people want to be a part of a church or other religious group that does community service and political activism. Unfortunately, most of these people aren't looking for a place to serve—they're really looking for someone else to do it so they can say "look what my church is doing," and Pagans aren't much different. Building a better, more just world here and now isn't the responsibility of a religious specialist. Service and activism are sacred work, but they're everyone's responsibility.

Academic research, theology, and philosophy aren't priestly work. For a religion or group of religions with so much emphasis on history and lore, research into history, anthropology, archaeology, and literature is sacred work. If you have skills in those areas and particularly have formal training and advanced degrees, a god may call you to put those skills to work for the benefit of our communities. That said, bardic work (singing and song writing, storytelling, writing fiction and non-fiction) isn't priestly work. Learning about old works is great, but so is creating new ones. My Pagan writing is part of my calling but a part that has nothing to do with priesthood.

Networking, relationship building, facility building, and maintenance are good and necessary, but they aren't priestly work. Somebody has to do all the mundane things it takes to build and maintain a community. Writing a ritual and organizing a public event are two separate skill sets. If this is your talent, put it to good use.

What is your calling? As you move beyond beginning practice, you are likely to hear a call to do something. The list of what you may be called to do includes many of the things Pagans and polytheists often are, but the list is by no means exclusive. That you are being called to do something by and for a god does not make it priesthood, and it does not make you a priest. Too many people are under the impression that giving regular devotion and worship to a god makes you their priest. It doesn't—it makes you their devotee. Being a devotee is a wonderful thing that should not be considered inferior to being a priest. The two are different, and they each carry different obligations and commitments. Listen for what you're being called to do. Then go do it to the best of your ability, whether it involves priesthood or not.

WHEN A GOD TURNS YOU UPSIDE DOWN

If we lived in a polytheist society, we would grow up learning the basics of polytheist belief and practice. When a god came calling, we would know the proper steps to take to discern who we were dealing with and what that meant. If we lived in a religiously neutral society, many of us (though not all) would end up as polytheists. While we might not know how to deal with an unexpected encounter with a god, at least we wouldn't have to unlearn a decade or five's worth of bad religion.

We don't live in either of those societies. We live in a society that's dominated by Christianity and its image of an all-powerful but very remote sky god who some say hasn't spoken to humanity in two-thousand years and others say speaks only through preachers. We live in a society where many people who claim to be Christians might as well be atheists for all the attention they pay to Jesus. We live in a society where a growing number of people are shouting that there are no gods at all. None of these things in any way prepares a person for the experience of having a god who may be limited in power but is still far bigger and stronger than us, suddenly grab us by the back of the neck and scream "you're mine." Because that happens too. And it can turn your world upside down.

Why do the gods approach us in such different ways? Why are they so gentle with some and so harsh with others? I don't know. All I know is that they do what they do for their own reasons. Our comfort (and at times, our sanity) doesn't appear to be too high on their list of priorities.

Who do the gods call or claim or grab? They rarely pick someone who isn't at least passingly familiar with them. There are enough of us now. They don't have to spend time and energy trying to "convert" someone who thinks they're demons or who thinks they're hallucinations. They can simply respond to those who've called on them. Polytheists I greatly respect have told me that the many gods are in fact omnipotent and omniscient. Perhaps, but I have serious doubts about that. And if, as I suspect, the gods can hear our thoughts but cannot read all the complicated emotions and convoluted reasoning behind them, I can imagine one of them having their own internal conversation that goes something like this:

"I need another priest (or warrior or organizer or Druid-on-retainer). Who can I call? Let's see, how about that person there? They asked me for help several times. I helped them out once, but I don't think they noticed. But they've got the skills I need, are capable of doing it, and seem like they're interested. I think I'll grab them."

If you're a long-time polytheist who's been pursuing a god for years, this may be a joyous day. If you're a new polytheist who's not quite sure what it's all about, it may be an awesome day—as in "full of awe." But if you've been told the gods are merely metaphors or archetypes, that the gods are all in your head, or that you can change your mind any time you like, this may be a day full of confusion and terror—or a week, a year, or the rest of your life.

Yes, we have sovereignty before the gods. Yes, we can say no. But what are you saying no to? Yourself? A metaphor? What happens when you try to reinterpret a myth and the "myth" resists reinterpretation? What happens when you insist the Morrígan is a nurturing mother goddess but all you receive are spears placed in your hands? What do you do when the beautiful stag becomes a raging beast?

What do you do when a god won't take "no" for an answer? What do you do if a god turns you upside down? What happens if you're a thirteen-year-old girl who is forcefully claimed by Hecate? What happens if you're a soldier in Afghanistan who among the snipers and mortars and land mines has a first-hand experience of the Morrígan? What happens if you're an agnostic nature-lover who runs face-first into Cernunnos in all his wild glory? Scott Cunningham's books aren't going to be much help.

My advice is to go with it. If an experience of a deity runs counter to your worldview, to your ideas about what is and isn't possible, just go with it. In the moment, and as you try to process it, do your best to accept that something you've always thought wasn't possible really happened. "There are more things in heaven and earth, Horatio, than are dreamt of in your philosophy." (*Hamlet*, Act I, scene v, 167–168) Don't try to force a religious experience into a materialist box. You can figure it all out later. For now, concentrate on what's happening, not how to interpret it.

Talk to them. Ask them what they want. Don't expect clear, explicit answers ... unless, of course, you get a clear explicit answer. And if you receive one, saying yes is probably the best thing to do. It's probably what you want to do, even if you don't know how you're going to do it, and even if it scares you silly. Unless it's something you can't do either literally or ethically (the gods' ethics are often different from ours which is usually a good reason to reexamine your own ethics). In which case, say what you can and will do. There's no guarantee your counteroffer will be accepted, but in my case it was.

Find someone to talk to who can relate to what happened, ideally a competent, experienced, polytheist priest. If you can find one in the tradition of the deity who grabbed you, so much the better. If you can't, find someone who at least understands the process. Your local tarot reader, UU minister, or witch isn't likely to be helpful unless, of course, they're also a polytheist priest. If you consult a mental health expert, find someone who understands the difference between mental illness and extreme religious experiences.

The direct experience of the gods can be an amazing, fulfilling, path-confirming experience. It can also be an ongoing experience of sheer terror. I can't tell you why it happens. I can't tell you why it hasn't happened to you. I can just tell you that it's happened to me, it's happened to others, and it seems to be happening more and more.

The gods are real. Our direct experiences of them are all the proof we need. But we often need help in interpreting our experiences and in figuring out how to go about doing what we've been "asked" to do. If a god turns you upside down, find someone who understands what's happened and talk with them.

Some religious experiences are so strong they force us to question our sanity. I'm a Druid and priest, not a psychologist; if you need mental health care, I can't help you. Get mental health care. That said, it is very rare for people to go from mostly functioning in the ordinary world to schizophrenic in the time it takes for a god to pick you up and throw you across the room. Irish author James Joyce once brought his daughter to see psychiatrist Carl Jung. Joyce didn't understand how his daughter could have schizophrenia. He said, "The way she thinks is the way I think, and I am not crazy." Jung's response was, "You are swimming. She is drowning."

Hearing a god and having mental health issues are not mutually exclusive; it's possible to have both. I have friends for whom it's both—their lives are challenging, to say the least. If you're drowning, get mental health care. But if you were swimming yesterday and today are face-to-face with a demanding deity, you're probably not going crazy. Rather, you're having a religious experience for which both our mainstream culture and much of the Pagan movement has no context. It's the lack of context that makes you think you're going crazy.

Go back over what happened—what did you perceive? What did you see, hear, feel, smell, taste, or otherwise notice? Your senses are not lying to you—you saw what you saw and heard what you heard. What thoughts popped into your head that weren't yours? Did you notice unfamiliar words, phrases, and concepts; things you had no way of knowing; or challenges to your ideas about what's important in life? Resist the urge to explain it away or worse, pretend it never happened. We can argue about how to interpret these experiences but that they happened is an objective fact. Figuring out what they mean requires locating them within the context of other experiences and within your ideas about the nature of the world and what is and isn't possible. And if you've read this far, the odds are you're starting to seriously question what you've always been taught about what is and isn't possible.

Our mainstream culture has no context for hearing a god. What happens when people who spend their whole lives in cities and suburbs are suddenly dropped in the wilderness? If it's a planned adventure with local guides and plenty of provisions, it can be a fun and educational experience. But if it's poorly planned, or especially if it's an emergency (car trouble, plane crash, etc.), it's stressful and scary and may be fatal. People who've lived their whole lives in cities and suburbs have no context for living in the wild.

If you relate your experience to a typical Protestant minister, they will most likely attempt to explain it in psychological terms because that's all they know. Most Pagans will do the same for the same reason. All they can imagine is that either you have a psychological issue or you're making it up. Their worldview doesn't include gods and spirits with sovereignty and agency—but that doesn't mean such beings don't exist.

Our ancient ancestors had context for perceiving the gods. Read the stories of the Greeks, Romans, and Norse. Read what the Egyptians quite literally carved in stone. Visit the remaining temples, burial chambers, and other sacred sites. While the gods were often inscrutable, it was understood that they were very real and were perfectly capable of turning the lives of humans upside-down. Plutarch was wrong—Pan is not dead. The gods of our ancestors may have faded into the background with the rise of monotheism, but for the past three-hundred years they've been becoming more and more active. Perhaps it would be better to say that we've started noticing them again, and sometimes we can't help but notice them.

Some cultures never lost contact with their gods. Hindus argue amongst themselves about whether Hinduism is polytheist or monotheist. I'm not a Hindu, but I see the worship of many gods, however you conceive of them. The African Traditional Religions have unbroken lineages that are thousands of years old, even though they're under attack from Christianity, Islam, and atheism. Context for the sudden firsthand experience of a god is available; we just have to dig a bit to find it.

Remember that the Big Tent of Paganism is a lousy first responder. I love the Big Tent of Paganism. It gives people like me who cannot stay in the mainstream religions an easy way to find all sorts of religious options. It helps diverse groups of practitioners come together for things like Pantheacon and The Wild Hunt. It encourages dialogue between people who are trying to build and rebuild religious traditions. But if you walk into the Big Tent with an urgent need for something that isn't Wicca or Witchcraft, you may not find what you need in time. This goes double if the first person you run into preaches the attractive but unhelpful idea that "deep down it's all the same" or "many paths, one mountain." This is why I fought efforts to define polytheism in nontheistic terms and continue to do so when necessary. Differences matter. If you're suddenly hearing a god, you need more than generic Paganism.

Ideally, you will find a priest of the god who's bothering you. That's likely to be difficult, however. For one thing, you may not know exactly who you've encountered, as many gods aren't big on identifying themselves at first contact. And even if you know who it is, it's not like there's a searchable directory of priests sorted by deity on the internet. Fortunately, there are a few things any competent priest (or priestess—I use "priest" inclusively, for a variety of reasons) in any polytheist tradition should be able to do.

They can provide spiritual first aid: grounding and shielding, prayers, and offerings. That will help you get back on your feet where you can start to process your experience. They can provide context. The Greek mythology you learned in high school is a start, but it's been filtered through centuries of Christian domination and decades of Hollywood exploitation. A polytheist priest can tell you how people experience the gods and understand them not two-thousand years ago but here and now. They can suggest resources. There are books that will help. Devotional practices are essential. And while whomever you speak to may not personally know a priest of the deity you're experiencing, they probably know someone who does. Networking isn't just a business thing. They can help you figure out how to interpret your experiences. People have come to me crying, "What does this mean?!" and I can't tell them—ultimately, you're the only one who can decide what your experiences mean. A competent priest, for their part, can ask helpful questions and point you in the right direction.

As an aside: if you consider yourself a priest or priestess and can't do all these things, learn. And learn quickly. When someone calls you out of the blue begging for help, you don't want to have to tell them, "I'm sorry, I didn't think I'd ever have a need for that skill."

Finally, respond to the call. In my experience, if a god is bothering you, it's not to make your life miserable. Neither is it to fix your problems and raise you up to some higher level. Rather, it's to call you into their service. What does that service look like? Anything that promotes their virtues and values in this world is a possibility, from private devotion to priesthood to public service and a hundred different alternatives. Whatever it is, it won't make your life easier. Serving the gods is work, and sometimes it's hot, dirty, and difficult work. But it will make your life deeper and more meaningful.

You must choose how to respond. I strongly recommend saying yes.

NEGOTIATING WITH THE GODS

What do you do when a deity comes calling that you do not want to serve? This is a more common question than you might think. For all the people who are craving more information about the Morrígan and are eager to join her service, I probably hear more reluctance about serving her than anyone else. I get it: she's intense, demanding, and never explains why she wants something done. She just wants it—now. And then there's the whole death and battle thing—stuff we don't like to think about. But it's not just the Morrígan; it's also Odin, it's Loki, it's even Cernunnos. It's not my place to judge. Many gods, many people, many relationships. So what do you do if a god calls you and you don't want to serve? There are multiple answers to this question; ultimately you have to figure out which one works for you.

You can say no. We all have sovereignty, even before the gods. We have the inherent right to make our own decisions and to choose our own course in life. The gods are not bound to respect our choices, as even a casual reading of the stories of our ancestors shows. Generally, however, they will accept refusal either out of respect or because it's easier for them to find someone who will say yes than to compel a reluctant devotee. If you really don't want to serve, you can say no, and maybe that will take care of it.

You can negotiate the terms of your service. Sometimes a deity will come to you with a specific request. More often, the request/demand is for open-ended service: to be a priest, devotee, messenger, or a Druid. Even in this situation, remember that there's nothing to stop you from narrowing the terms of your service. Offer specifics: "I will do this but not that," "I will make these offerings but not those," "I will commit to you for a year but after that we renegotiate," and so on. Honestly, unless you already have an established informal relationship and have built up a relationship, I recommend negotiating terms. Do not assume their goals line up with your goals. I've generally been successful in negotiating terms of service but not always.

You can fall back on prior commitments. While we have sovereignty, we are not the gods' equals. We do not have their age, experience, wisdom, or virtue—or, most relevantly to this, their power. If you fight a god and they care about winning, you will lose. It helps to have powerful allies. I've told several Norse deities no. In one case I was backed up by those to whom I am oathed, who said "this one is ours and we're keeping him plenty busy." I think there was a "for now" at the end of that sentence, but I'll worry about that when I have to. On the other hand, the Morrígan is known to engage in horse trading with Odin, so this doesn't always work.

You can call in outside counsel. If you aren't up for it yourself, call in a priest of the deity in question to do divination and negotiate for you. If a god is calling you and you want to say no, odds are that you don't know them well. And let's face it—communication with deities isn't as straightforward as picking up the phone or sending an e-mail. Miscommunication is easy. A priest or other person acquainted with that god is much more likely to be able to ascertain requests/demands at a more specific level. They are also more likely to be able to communicate your concerns in a clear manner. I've done this on several occasions with good results, though not always the results I wanted.

If a deity wants you badly enough to be persistent, it may be in your best interests to say yes. Not just because they can make your life miserable if you don't (although that's always a possibility), but because they may want or need you for something important, something that deep down you want to be a part of, even if it scares you. The Morrígan is many things, but I have never found her to be petty—if she wants you, there's a good reason. She scares me at times, but I have always found her to be honorable and have always been glad I was able to contribute to the work to which she called me.

You may not have a choice. It's not often that a deity ignores a person's requests and claims them forcefully, but it happens. If that's you and your situation, re-read When a God Turns You Upside Down.

Why do the gods choose us? I'll leave the ethical and metaphysical reasons to the philosophers and theologians, but what I know is this: there are always reasons. Something needs to be done and a specific person is the best (or possibly the only) one to do it. That person will be needed for something down the road and preparations have to start now. Or maybe they're just caught up in the Otherworldly version of the military draft.

If a deity calls you and you don't want to serve, you have several options. Start working through them and see if you can come to an arrangement that works for you.

THIS ISN'T THE KOBAYASHI MARU: WHEN YOU HAVE TO BREAK A GEAS

A *geas* is a religious obligation or prohibition. It's an Irish word, sometimes spelled *geis* or *géis*; the plural is *geasa*. A geas can come from many sources, but most often it's placed upon a person by a god or by a spiritually powerful person. The ultimate purpose of a geas is often mysterious. Is it to keep them away from danger so they can fulfill a later purpose? Is it to lift their reputation as a virtuous person? Or is it to doom them to an early death? Geasa are rarely explained.

The great hero Cú Chulainn had two geasa: one to never refuse hospitality when offered, and another to never eat dog meat. So when an old woman offered him a piece of the dog she was cooking, he was in a no-win situation. He ate the dog and lost strength on one side of his body. This weakened him to the point he was finally defeated in combat and killed.

In the *Star Trek* universe, the Kobayashi Maru is a test at Starfleet Academy. In it, the cadet is placed in a command simulation in a no-win situation. It is not designed to test how the cadet solves problems but how they respond to stress. It is a test of character and composure. For the non-geek readers of this book, there was one cadet who defeated the Kobayashi Maru: James T. Kirk. Kirk reprogrammed the testing computers so it was possible to win. When challenged on it, he said he didn't believe in no-win situations.

Those of us who carry geasa, taboos, and other religious obligations and prohibitions can sometimes find ourselves in situations that feel like the Kobayashi Maru. Sometimes multiple geasa can be in conflict. Sometimes keeping a geas means violating an ethical principle. Sometimes it places a great burden on ourselves or on those close to us. But this is not the Kobayashi Maru. There is no testing computer to reprogram. The damage done is not simulated. No-win situations aren't fair, but they exist, and we need to be prepared for them.

If you think you have to break a geas, first make sure it's *really* a geas. I was once contacted by someone asking for advice about breaking a geas. After reflection, they determined that the obligation they had was neither a geas placed upon them nor a vow freely made, but a badge they wished to wear. It was a self-imposed restriction to tell themselves and others "how special and awesome I am" (an exact quote, used with permission). Recognizing the source of that obligation was a good step forward. It is not having a geas but living virtuously—with or without a geas—that makes a person special and awesome.

Geasa may be placed on you in a dramatic and straightforward fashion, or you may come into them more subtly. Some come along with initiations and formal relationships with certain gods and spirits. Some are placed on an entire family or tribe. Figuring out if you have a geas requires understanding your heritage and your tradition. Oftentimes it requires divination. And sometimes, as in the example above, it requires knowing yourself.

Do you really have to break it? If you have a geas against eating a particular food or foods, it is unlikely you will ever have to break it. You may have to skip some tasty looking dishes, and in certain circumstances may end up with a rather meager meal. But the worst problem you're likely to have is telling a host, "I'm sorry, my religion doesn't permit me to eat that," which most people will understand. Those who push are rude, and you don't owe them a further explanation.

On the other hand, food prohibitions are easy to break unintentionally: ingredients aren't always fully disclosed. Commercial food suppliers are required by law to disclose ingredients, but your aunt who makes those wonderful stews and pies isn't. "I didn't know what I was eating" isn't an acceptable excuse.

Vegans abstain from all animal products. Devout Muslims pray five times every day, regardless of what else is going on. Amish fashion choices are extremely limited. I would not call any of these obligations geasa, but they are all examples of how religious obligations are fulfilled day in and day out by ordinary people. Think hard. You may be inconvenienced or stand out more than you'd prefer, but you probably don't have to break your geas.

Remember to read the fine print. Take a lesson from our friends the Fair Folk: are there creative ways you can fulfill your geas? The idea that you must always fulfill the spirit of an obligation and not simply its letter is not universally shared, and not just by the Good Neighbors. If you have a geas to always offer hospitality to anyone who asks and a Nazi knocks on your door, just how far are you required to go? If a Nazi is starving I'll find something for him to eat, but I'm not offering him a prime cut of roast beef. If you're forbidden to wear a hat and it's going to be dangerously cold, can you wear a hood?

I try to stay within the spirit of an obligation in part because that's what our society expects and in part because I don't want someone else invoking the fine print on me (reciprocity, reciprocity, reciprocity). But if there's a choice between breaking a geas and fulfilling it on a fine distinction, I'd rather keep it. Just make sure you stay on the right side of the fine print. If in doubt, do divination or consult a qualified diviner.

Can you negotiate a temporary exception? Let's say you've pored over the situation for days. It really is a geas, you really do have to break it, and there are no loopholes that provide a workable exception. Now what? Perhaps the person who created the geas (and here I use "person" in the animistic sense, which includes god persons and spirit persons as well as human persons) has an interest in whatever it is you need to do that would require breaking the geas. Perhaps they would temporarily suspend the geas, under certain circumstances or with certain conditions. You won't know unless you ask.

Do not presume a favorable response. You must ask, and you must receive an affirmative answer. If the person in question isn't a human person, that means divination is required. Even if the person who gave you the geas wants to make an exception, they may be unable. Geasa are magical operations, and once started they can take on a life of their own.

Still no luck? Do the best you can to smooth things over. Before the act that will break the geas, make propitiatory offerings—and don't skimp on the quality or quantity. Afterwards, make additional offerings and perform rites of purification appropriate for your tradition and your circumstances. If you aren't sure what's appropriate, consult a qualified diviner or a priest of your tradition. Much of the knowledge and technology around geasa and other religious prohibitions has been lost over the centuries of Christian domination. We're rebuilding it, but the process is slow. Few ordinary practitioners understand these things, and even priests may need to refer you to other priests. But it's ultimately better to spend the time (and if necessary, money) to get it right than to guess about a sacred obligation and get it wrong.

I have two relatively minor geasa. Breaking them would not result in my death. But what it takes to make things right if they are broken is in many ways far more expensive than keeping them, so there is never a temptation to try to buy my way around them. If I do, somehow, it is still possible to make amends.

If all else fails, die valiantly. Cú Chulainn ate the dog meat, broke his geas, and became critically weakened. However, he still went into battle as his honor demanded. When his wounds became too great, he tied himself to a standing stone facing the enemy so he could die on his feet with his sword in his hand. Sometimes the measure of a person is found not in clever strategies to win, but in living honorably and virtuously in defeat.

ORACULAR LEADERSHIP

If Pagans have models of what religious community looks like, odds are good those models come from other religions: for example, a Christian church centered around a priest or a minister who leads worship and provides spiritual guidance for the community. It's certainly not the only way, however. Even in a group of polytheists committed to the devout worship of their gods, a priest is unlikely to have the authority to make the kind of unilateral decisions made by Christian pastors. A different way is needed.

Oracular leadership is leading—yourself, other individuals, and communities—based on revelation from gods and spirits. The closest term I know is "prophetic leadership" (which I've used before,) but that term comes from Jewish and Christian traditions—I'd rather use a term with polytheist roots.

Revelations can come through yourself, or other oracles, mystics, and priests. It can come through collaboration with diviners, but ultimately its source is Otherworldly. We tend to take messages from gods and spirits very seriously—or at least I do and recommend you do as well, even if you choose to do something other than what you're being asked or told to do. We have sovereignty before the gods, but that sovereignty is best exercised mindfully and fully informed.

As Pagans and polytheists, we like to point out the irony of people whose god just so happens to hate all the same people they hate. Distinguishing Otherworldly messages from our own thoughts is very difficult, even when we're trying hard to keep them separate. Some religions claim to avoid this problem by grounding themselves in holy books. There certainly is value in the accumulated wisdom of a religious tradition (including wisdom kept in an oral tradition), but this sort of justification only moves the goal posts. All sacred texts began as someone's private revelation.

Those of us who receive this kind of communication soon learn that other people don't always take these messages as seriously as we'd like. That's understandable. Having a deity merge with your being provides a level of authenticity that hearing another person say, "Danu told me to tell you this" can never duplicate.

But the gods do not always limit their wisdom, their requests, and their demands to individuals. Sometimes they have something to say to a group or a community, and those of us who are their oracles have the responsibility to lead based on that revelation. And that presents a whole new set of challenges. This is particularly difficult when an oracular leader is also an administrative leader, as frequently happens in small Pagan groups. There is the risk that in the zeal to accomplish a divinely-mandated task, a leader will abuse their human authority. They may eschew established processes, hog limited resources, and generally ignore the needs and desires of other members of the group.

On the other hand is the risk of self-censorship. The oracular/administrative leader may decide that doing what they've been asked to do might upset some people, so in an effort to keep the peace they fail to deliver a message or lead the group in a direction it really needs to go.

I see five qualities an oracular leader must have in order to meet these challenges.

DISCERNMENT

Discernment is the ability and willingness to distinguish one thing from another. In this case, it means the ability and willingness to separate the voices of the gods from your own voice. That's the biggest challenge in any oracular work, whether you're taking omens before leading a cattle raid or if you're just reading tarot at the local psychic fair. Good discernment begins with knowing yourself. If you know what's you, it's a lot easier to recognize what's not you. What thoughts, what feelings, what ideas are yours? Not everything the gods and spirits tell us is contrary to what we'd like it to be, but the closer our messages are to our own preferences, the more skeptical we need to be. Recognizing the "other" voice gets easier and more reliable with time and practice, but it's never certain. Practicing good discernment is always necessary.

DIPLOMACY

An oracular leader must be a diplomat. Our gods are not infallible, and while participating in their work is usually both helpful and rewarding, sometimes their requests aren't compatible with our contemporary world. The Morrigan sometimes makes requests more suitable for the Iron Age than the Information Age. In any case, unquestioning faith is not a Pagan virtue. Sometimes we need to negotiate with the gods as to what we can do, what we will do, and what's just not going to happen.

We also have to be diplomatic with the groups we lead. Announcing "the Dagda wants us to do this" isn't likely to carry much weight with a group of eclectic Pagans. It may not carry much weight with a group of Celtic polytheists if they aren't used to hearing such messages, or if they've got other ideas about what should be done. Translating the desires of the gods into things people can do and will do requires serious thought and a careful choice of words.

PATIENCE

This is hard for me, because I have no patience. The gods are immortal— I'm not (at least not in this lifetime). But some things will either happen in their own time or not at all. It takes time for people to go from hearing something new to accepting it. It takes time for organizations to change and grow. The grand temples of antiquity weren't built in a day, or in a year, or in some cases, in a century. Sometimes the people needed to accomplish what you've been asked to do aren't there with you yet. All you can do is lay the groundwork and try to provide good hospitality when they show up so as not to run them off before they ever get involved. Patience is not procrastination. Don't worry about what you can't do yet— work diligently on what you can do now.

FLEXIBILITY

One of the core principles of effective magic is to work for the desired end result, not the method of getting there. If you need a new job, you might find it on a job search site, you might find it through a friend, you might find it through a recruiter, or you might find a way to become self-employed. Limiting yourself to just one approach reduces the chances you'll find something suitable. Likewise, if you're leading based on revelation from gods and spirits, there are likely many ways to get to where they want you to go. If some approaches are more doable than others, use them. If some are more appealing to your group, use them. Accomplishing what you've been told to accomplish is the main thing—how you accomplish it is just details.

COMMITMENT

Good, authentic, oracular leadership requires a commitment to the messages the gods send us. That means doing all the things you're reading about in this section. Some things can't be compromised; sometimes one or two details really are that important. Sometimes a call to be patient is just someone stalling in hopes that you'll give up. At the same time, "the gods told me to" is no excuse for violating the trust of others or for abandoning the obligations you accepted as an administrative leader. If you can't do what you've been told to do without running over the rest of the group, then you have to find another way, sometimes with a sub-group: "I'm doing this—who wants to do it with me?" (while maintaining your obligations to the whole group). Sometimes it means finding a second group in addition to your primary group. Sometimes it means striking out on your own.

Ideally, administrative leadership and oracular leadership would be separate. The Christian corollary is a church where a lay board of trustees manages the operations and the pastor provides the spiritual leadership, as opposed to the megachurch model where the pastor *is* the CEO. Small Pagan groups may not have the resources for such separation of powers, but the risk of conflict and of conflict of interest is reduced where possible.

Some messages from the gods are mysteries to be pondered. Others are orders that require a deep commitment to do what you've been asked to do, no matter what it costs. Oracular leadership is difficult, but if it's what you've been called to do, do it as honestly and effectively as you can.

11

BUILDING DEEP
RELIGIOUS COMMUNITIES

FEW THINGS ARE AS guaranteed to get a negative response than talking with Pagans about the need for community. For all that the story of
modern Paganism is the story of traditions, orders, and lineages, our
growth has largely come through solitary practitioners. Some of us are
isolated, some have had bad experiences in religious groups (Pagan or
otherwise), and some of us just don't like working with other people.
But while your practice can be completely solitary, it makes things
harder than they would otherwise be.

In *The Earth, The Gods, and The Soul: A History of Pagan Philosophy from the Iron Age to the 21st Century,* Brendan Myers demonstrates
that despite the complete dominance of Christianity in the medieval
era, Pagan ideas did not disappear entirely but because there were no
Pagan institutions—no Pagan communities—the few people interested
in Pagan ideas simply rehashed the same things over and over again.
It was only with the rise of Pagan groups in the twentieth century that

Paganism became a living tradition once again. Pagan communities are not just about celebrating the sabbats together or even about forming mutually supportive friendships with your co-religionists; they're also about magical workings that require more than one person to perform. They're about people who will hold us accountable for doing the things we said we were going to do. They're about people with whom we can confidently share our most intimate religious experiences and know they'll understand. And perhaps most importantly for those of us engaging in deeper practices, Pagan communities are about challenging our interpretations of those experiences and encouraging us to think longer and harder about them, and in doing so get closer to the truth of the matter.

There are Wiccan covens and generic Pagan groups in virtually every city and town. As of this writing, Ár nDraíocht Féin (ADF) has sixty-four groves and protogroves around the United States, and the Covenant of Unitarian Universalist Pagans (CUUPS) has around seventy chapters and related groups. Other orders and traditions have fewer groups but are out there—you won't know till you look. You may have to drive a bit (or possibly a lot) or work with a group that's not in your preferred tradition, but with a little digging you can find a group to work with.

Finding a group that does the kind of deep work we're discussing in this book is another matter altogether. There aren't very many, even in large cities. And the deeper you go, the more important it becomes to work with someone in your specific tradition. There are some Western Mystery Tradition orders that do some very deep work, but that won't do if you're a devotional polytheist.

The first place to start is online. Perhaps you can find a group that's doing exactly what you're trying to do. There are countless Facebook groups for such things, but sadly most are anything but deep. But it is possible to find a series of individuals like yourself who are doing the best they can working on their own and with "communities of convenience" that provide companionship but not much spiritual help. These individuals can become the basis for a virtual community. You can meet people at conferences, conventions, and retreats. Even if your travel budget is limited, there is probably something within your means, even if you can only do one a year or even one every two or three years.

And then there's the old saying, "If you want something done right, do it yourself." Perhaps you need to start your own Pagan study group, meditation group, or magical practice group. Perhaps you need to create a virtual temple to your patron deity and look for others to help you write and perform devotions. Perhaps you need to formally found a new Pagan religious order. The first option is fairly simple, the second is more complicated, and the third is beyond the scope of this book.

However you decide to build your Pagan religious community, there are some things to keep in mind.

THE CAULDRON OF THE DAGDA: PROVIDING HOSPITALITY

In Irish mythology, the Cauldron of the Dagda is one of the Four Hallows of the Tuatha De Danann. No company ever went away from it unfilled. No matter how many people needed to be fed, there was always enough food for everyone. The Cauldron has taken many forms over the centuries, but in this original form it was a means of hospitality—a tool for providing food to guests.

Ordinary hospitality is the process of making guests feel welcome and taking care of their needs. It is one of the core virtues of Paganism and of humanity in general. The Proto-Indo-European word *ghosti* is the root of the English words for both guest and host, pointing toward the shared obligations of both. In the ancient world, hospitality frequently meant opening your home to strangers. Travel was slow and dangerous and in many places accommodations simply didn't exist.

Sleeping outdoors left travelers vulnerable to the elements, wild animals, and human predators. Food and water could be difficult or impossible to find. Particularly in harsh environments, refusing hospitality was tantamount to saying "I don't care if you live or die." Providing hospitality was and is a sign of respect for others and their inherent worth.

Pagan groups sometimes struggle with providing hospitality to our visitors. We forget about the strangers who went to the trouble of coming to our event and spend all our free time talking with our friends. But with mindfulness and some good processes, we can show proper hospitality to all. In natural disasters and the related evacuations, the need for ordinary hospitality is re-emphasized: some need temporary housing and short-term assistance until they can return to their homes. Others need long-term assistance rebuilding their lives.

Although the need for ordinary hospitality is great, another form of hospitality—spiritual hospitality—has great need too. Many times, people show up at our doors (literally or metaphorically) looking for something less tangible than a bowl of stew. They're looking for help dealing with the big questions of life. They had an encounter with a god or a spirit and need help figuring out what to do next. They're on a spiritual journey, and fate or chance or the gods themselves brought them to you. They need hospitality every bit as much as those in need of physical sustenance. How can we provide it? Is there a Cauldron of the Dagda for spiritual hospitality?

First, you need a way for people to find you. You can be the most competent and generous host in the world, but that won't do any good if people can't find you. Does your group have a website, Facebook page, or a Twitter account? A booth at Pagan Pride Day? A presence at regional and national gatherings?

There are some traditions who see finding them as an ordeal in and of itself: "if you're supposed to find us, you'll find us." I respect that approach if there's some thought and intention behind it. But if you're not an occult (i.e., "hidden") group, that's not tradition, only laziness and inhospitality.

Make it clear who you are and who you aren't. Lots of people say "everyone is welcome" but no one really means it. At Denton CUUPS' rituals, we say "we welcome all who come in love and friendship." Nazis aren't welcome. White supremacists aren't welcome. Open-minded Christians and Nature-centered non-theists are very welcome; fundamentalists of any persuasion aren't.

Nobody takes everybody. When some people say, "Everyone is welcome" what they really mean is, "We want everyone to come so we can change them to be just like us," which isn't practicing hospitality, it's proselytizing. Beyond these (hopefully) obvious examples, you can't be everything to everyone, even as a generic Pagan group. If your emphasis is nature spirituality and environmental activism, say so. If it's devotional polytheism, say so. If it's Gardnerian Wicca, say so. It is not inhospitable to say, "We don't do what you're looking for." Of course, saying so means you have to know who you are.

What do you teach? Once you know who you are, you can start figuring out what you need to teach. That process begins with understanding that you can't teach what you don't know. Maybe you can "stay one lesson ahead" on some subjects, but magic and religion aren't on that list.

What do you know well enough to teach? What's important enough to you or your group that you need to teach it? What are the foundational principles, the core practices, and the experiences someone needs to have along the way?

How will you teach? Some witchcraft traditions teach one-to-one, face-to-face, which is an excellent way to learn, but it's not the only way. Classes can be held in person or online. OBOD has one of the best teaching systems in the world, and not just the Pagan world. They still operate as a postal-mail correspondence course. Many (probably most) contemporary Pagans have done the bulk of their learning from books. I've learned much of what I know by diving in head first and learning by doing. There are many ways to teach. Choose the one(s) that match your material, your teaching skills, and your students' needs.

Ask what your guests need, and then listen. Are they in spiritual trauma? Do they need magical first aid? Or do they need more mundane assistance?

Sometimes you have to turn people away because you don't offer what they need. Sometimes you need to refer them to another group: if you're a devotional polytheist group and they want non-theistic nature spirituality, point them in the right direction. Sometimes they need what you have, but not exactly in the way you've been doing it. We are not fundamentalists—no one way is right for everyone. Don't be so eager to teach a newcomer that you fail to discern whether they really need what you can offer.

Do you have secrets? Of course you do. Maybe you have sacred names, deep mysteries, or rituals involving great vulnerability. These must not be profaned (i.e., "made ordinary") by letting them become widely known. They're usually guarded with careful protocols and with dread oaths. Or perhaps your secrets are hidden in plain sight. Perhaps your secrets are something special about the culture of your group: a food you always eat, a color you always wear (or never wear), a song that has a special meaning no one can describe but everyone knows is important. When the time comes to share these secrets, how will you transmit them? Revealing them by telling them is perhaps the least effective method. How can people uncover these secrets and experience them for themselves?

We can argue for days and days about whether or not groups or individuals have power they can transmit to new initiates, but it's part of many traditions. And this issue isn't unique to Pagans, either; Christians have been arguing over apostolic succession for centuries. In some forms of Wicca, the initiator places one hand on the candidate's head and the other on their foot and wills their power into them. Does that accomplish anything? I can't say because I've never tried it. But I clearly remember the moment of investiture at my first Pagan initiation. Something powerful happened, and it felt right.

I tend to think the initiators in these cases aren't the source so much as they're the facilitators and the conduits. The magic, the power, the current (call it what you will) flows through them and into the candidate. If your tradition has such a feature, you need a way to transmit it.

Hospitality is a form of reciprocity: someone helped you get started. Maybe it was a teacher, an author, an artist, or nature herself. Because someone showed you hospitality, you learned, grew, and became more than what you were before. If guests knock on your door, it means you've done something to get the attention of someone … or Someone. You have been a guest. Now it's time to be a host.

NORMAL OR WEIRD—WE NEED BOTH

A while back I had a conversation with a fellow Pagan priest who, like me, holds down a job in the corporate world. This priest was having some difficulties with members of their local group who were giving the person a hard time about being "too normal." It was intended to be good-natured kidding (we think) but it cut a little too deeply.

When I talk about the "Big Tent of Paganism" I usually mean making room for different religious and spiritual traditions and approaches: Wicca, Druidry, and Heathenry, polytheism, pantheism, and atheism. It includes and accepts nature-centered, deity-centered, self-centered, and community-centered forms of worship. The Big Tent also needs to be big enough to accommodate different personalities, lifestyles, and occupations. Everybody has to chop wood and carry water—our Paganism needs to have room for plumbers and accountants as well as for mystics and priests.

I function quite well in the mainstream world. I wish I didn't have to, but it's a game and life is easier if you can figure out how to play the game well. A good society needs a healthy mixture of "normal" people who keep the lights on, and "weird" people who constantly challenge them to do better. Some of us manage to keep a foot in both worlds.

If we can be accepting of different races, genders, and sexual orientations, we can be accepting of people who are "weird," "normal," and everything in between. We need the people who navigate the mainstream world with ease just as much as those who follow the beat of a different drummer. We need the people with strong organizational skills, and we need those who constantly challenge organizational norms. We need the outgoing and the introverted, the hard-shelled and the sensitive, the musicians and the engineers, the radicals and the soccer moms, and those who are their own unique blend of all of the above.

And all these people who hear the call of the gods, of nature, and of magic need the support and encouragement of their fellow Pagans and the Pagan community. Let's accept people for who and what they are, even if they're weird … and even if they're not. Let's build our Pagan culture around the virtues of hospitality and reciprocity, not around rejecting—or accepting—mainstream appearances.

12

THE COST OF
DEEP PRACTICE

WEEKLY OFFERINGS AND DEVOTIONS are a part of my regular spiritual practice. Sunday evening is for the Morrígan, Monday is for my ancestors, and Wednesday is for Cernunnos. Tuesday is for someone I don't talk about publicly. I say a prayer of invocation, make offerings (usually a libation), and then listen. This is the most intimate time of my regular practice.

Some weeks I hear nothing. Most weeks I hear something along the lines of "keep doing the work." And sometimes I've heard, "It's time to go deeper and to get further away from distractions." I am not the only one hearing this call.

What is it you want most? Our individual desires stand in an interesting spot. On one hand, the wants of any one particular creature are ultimately irrelevant. On the other hand, our wants motivate us to work toward them, and that often helps advance the greater good. While there is value in the Christian idea of self-denial and in the Buddhist idea of non-attachment, at the end of the day you'll do best at something you're passionate about. That deep desire keeps you going when things get hard or when a routine has to be maintained day in and day out. Desire means you will spend more time thinking about something, practicing it, and playing with it, which means your knowledge and skills will grow. It is honorable and virtuous to do what must be done even though you don't want to do it. Yet there is very little in life that truly must be done, and most of that is simply keeping the commitments you have already made.

What I want most right now is to continue exploring the depths of Pagan and polytheist devotion and magic. As a kid I wanted to be a baseball player. I played two years of Little League and found I was really bad at it. Sometimes wanting isn't enough. As an adult, I wanted to be a corporate executive. I got on the track to advance in the corporate world and found I didn't like it. If at some time in my late twenties you told me I'd find happiness as a Druid, priest, and writer, I would have laughed at you. I always wanted to be a writer, but I thought a writer was someone who stayed home all day and made millions of dollars. The idea that I'd gladly spend countless hours at the keyboard for a fraction of minimum wage (let alone even more countless hours doing religious work for no pay) was unthinkable. Yet here I am. I'm a Pagan because I started reading Wicca 101 books and casting simple spells for silly reasons. I'm a Druid because Wicca didn't work for me and I decided to try something different. I'm a priest because I had an ecstatic experience of the Forest God and wanted to learn as much from it as I could (and because I wanted to do it again). I'm a writer because I wanted to work through some religious issues and I started a blog on a free blogging site. And I'm not a kabbalist or a religious scholar or a UU minister because I took steps down those paths and figured out fairly quickly I didn't have much passion for them.

What is it you think you want? Go for it. It's OK to fail, but fail fast and learn from your failures. Sooner or later you'll hit the one you really want. Exploration and experimentation are part of the cost that must be paid for what we want most. I didn't know deep, animistic, magical, polytheism existed when I started. But I've come far enough down this path to discover my passion for it.

What are you trying to bring along for the ride? Very few of us are single-minded. Even if we know where our passion lay and we're committed to it, there are still other things in life we want and need. "Balance" is often a cliché in the Pagan community (or worse, an excuse for mediocrity), but a local friend once relayed a message to me: "too much speed and too much effort without rest will kill the vintner as well as the wine."

There's a reason some monastic orders live lives of such simplicity they border on deprivation: they want to eliminate as many distractions as possible from their worship and contemplation. We need not copy their rules exactly, but the fact remains that there are only so many hours in a day. Some must be devoted to rest. Some must be devoted to relaxation, to enjoying "guilty pleasures" for which we should feel no guilt, because they offer a bit of joy and help us go back to our life's work with a fresh start. Beyond that, secondary concerns distract us from our true passions. Do you enjoy a couple of TV shows, or is your life tied up in fictional universes and the mundane lives of celebrities? Do you enjoy good food or are you obsessed with cooking and restaurants? Are you a responsible citizen or are you obsessed with politics? There's something to be said for dressing well, but Steve Jobs wore the same black turtleneck and jeans every day because it was one less thing to distract him from the work he wanted to concentrate on.

I'm not saying there are "good" and "bad" activities or even saying moderation is key. The matter here is a question of time management. The more hours you spend on secondary passions, the fewer hours you have to spend on primary passions.

There are some interests in my life that are good and healthy and enjoyable, but I've had to have to cut them back (or rather, crowd them out) because they were taking time away from my deepest callings. This is part of the cost that must be paid. What is taking time away from your deep passion and your great work?

When you're getting started, remember that something is better than nothing. Deep callings do not come to us fully formed. We have an image or an idea of what it will look and feel like, but until we start doing it, we don't really know what all is involved. Yet too many of us look at these imagined end states, realize we can't get there right away, and conclude it's hopeless. And so instead of doing something that will move us closer to our goal, we despair and do nothing, which is not just a problem for beginners.

I have a vision of where my deeper work will take me, but it is vague and obscured. I can't create a detailed project plan with timelines and checkpoints. All I can do is start walking in that direction with the realization that I may not get there (where ever *there* is) in this lifetime.

Our mainstream culture talks about "having faith" that everything will work out OK even if we have no reason to expect it will. Pagans aren't big on that kind of faith. But we can be faithful to the callings of our gods and ancestors, and trust that doing something will be good and helpful, even if it may not be everything we wish it was.

There is a very utilitarian ethic to spiritual practice: do the work and you get the benefits. Don't do the work and you won't. Oftentimes the gods are gracious and give us things we have not earned. Their generosity is a virtue we would do well to emulate. But some things cannot be given, only obtained through sustained effort. No one could give me the experience of running a marathon or the wisdom I gained in doing it. I cannot command the presence of the gods in my life, but without years of devotional practice I would rarely hear them, much less understand what they're telling me. Whether you want to be a marathon runner or a magician, a concert pianist or a priest, there is a high cost to being the best you can be. The down payment is due in advance and the ongoing payments never end. I have found them to be the best investments I've ever made.

There is plenty of room in Paganism and polytheism for people who simply want to honor the gods and live good ordinary lives with no interest in deep practice. But some of us are called to deep devotional and magical practice. We are called to go off the map and draw new ones for those who come after us.

Some of us want these things very, very much. They do not come for free; there is a cost to be paid, and that cost is often high—sometimes extremely high. I intend to pay it because it is what I want most. I don't think I'm the only one.

THE MONSTERS THAT LIVE IN THE DEPTHS

Some people simply aren't interested in deep practice. Some are committed to a worldview that does not allow for things like gods, spirits, and fae. Some are at the very early stages of their Pagan practice and aren't yet ready for deeper practice. If you're reading this book, that probably isn't you. If you're reading this book, you probably feel the call to deeper and perhaps darker practices but may be afraid of them. You may have experienced something that was more real than expected and now you're leery of continuing.

Then there are those who rush into dealings with spiritual beings with all the caution of a college student leaving a party with a blood alcohol content of 0.15 and insistence they can drive themselves home just fine.

Fear isn't always a bad thing. Humans have an innate fear of snakes, as do other primates. That fear helps us avoid dying painful deaths after being bitten by venomous snakes. Problems arise when reasonable fears become unreasonable ... and when reasonable fears cannot be avoided.

There are things in the depths that can harm us. There are also treasures in the depths. Ferí co-founder Victor Anderson said that "anything worthwhile is dangerous." Our job is to evaluate the risks calmly and accurately. This will allow us to avoid risks that carry little reward, mitigate risks that are necessary, and be prepared for risks that play out in ways that are difficult or harmful.

Good horror writers—as opposed to those who write gore or torture porn—understand that the less you show, the scarier it is. The unknown is humanity's greatest fear.

If we grew up in a society where concepts like animism, polytheism, and magic were part of the culture, deep practice wouldn't be so scary. Like our ancestors, we would learn from birth how to approach the gods, interact with the fae, and work spells and charms. Sadly, we don't live in that society. Most of our neighbors ignore such concepts and beings, while those of us who are drawn to them are left trying to figure out where the boundaries are, what's a real risk, and what's an ordinary bug magnified to a hundred feet tall by our imagination.

The best way to combat the fear of the unknown is to make it known. Read, study, and practice. Working in a group means you have other resources at hand or someone to say, "I don't think that bug is a hundred feet tall." If you can work with an experienced person, you've got someone who can say, "I've never seen a hundred-foot bug and the ten-foot bugs only hang out in certain areas that are easily avoided." But if you never open the door, you'll never know.

Then there are the monsters within. I believe the gods and spirits are real, distinct, individual beings. Attempts to understand them in purely psychological terms are insufficient to explain my experiences and the experiences of many others. But that doesn't mean the psychological explanations of spirits and magic are completely wrong—they aren't. There are metaphorical monsters living inside each and every one of us. As much as we like to think we're good, compassionate, non-violent people, each of us has the capacity to do great evil—particularly when an authority figure tells us to do it. Mostly we don't think about these things, and that's mostly a good idea. The New Age concept that what we dwell on we will manifest is more true than not true. But like most everything else we don't like, ignoring them won't make them go away.

In order to do deep spiritual work, you must first know yourself. This is one of the reasons so many magical orders focus on self-discovery and self-development. (Too many people never get past the emphasis on the self, but that's another rant for another day.) When you examine your inner self, your deep self, you are likely to find monsters—and monsters are scary.

Some people refuse to ever open that door. They slam the door shut and go back to pretending they're made of nothing but light and love. I want to know what's living inside me. I want to know exactly what these monsters are. Some are my evolutionary heritage from ancestors most ancient. Some are the product of my upbringing and early childhood experiences. Some I don't know where they come from, I just know they're there. Some monsters can be reasoned with. Some can be healed. Some can be constrained with prayers and magic. With wise and diligent practice, we can keep our monsters from harming ourselves and others.

Some monsters I prefer to keep around. As much as we try to make the world a kinder, gentler place, it often isn't. There are times when monsters are necessary. But I can do none of that if I'm afraid to take a cold hard look at the monsters within.

Some of the scary things we encounter in deeper practice are parts of ourselves. Others aren't. Over the past couple of years, I've had first-hand encounters with gods, ancestors, fae, spirits, and things I can't classify and won't try. I've worked magic for a very long time (even if I wouldn't have called it that at first) and I've seen results I can't deny. I'm at the point where it's easier to just go with it than try to rationalize it away... and I like it better that way anyway. Not all these experiences have been positive, however. Some have been rather unpleasant. Practice deeply enough for long enough and you'll come to the realization that wherever humans are in the grand scheme of things, it's not at the top. Even if the gods are virtuous (and they are) they aren't particularly interested in your comfort and security. And there are plenty of beings out there that aren't nearly as virtuous as the gods.

I've done a lot of hiking over the course of my life. Most of it has been in relatively safe places, but some has been in wild places where large and carnivorous wild animals live. It can be dangerous wandering into bear or cougar territory, but those animals live in some of the most beautiful and magical places on earth. If you know a bit about wild animals and show them some respect, they'll mostly leave you alone. They won't be your teachers and they certainly won't be your servants, but they'll allow you to pass unmolested through their territory to do what you came to do.

Some monsters are like wild animals. Others are more like your next-door neighbor who yells when your leaves blow into his yard, but who was quite friendly the time you brought him an apple pie. And others defy comparison.

As with all relationships, our dealings with Otherworldly beings must be grounded in respect, reciprocity, and honor. Be impeccable with your word, and do not offer or promise what you cannot or will not do.

If you practice deeply enough for long enough, you will encounter beings whose very presence will scare you. Let your fear teach you how to be a good explorer, not how to stay on the couch. Another world is out there, and if you've read this far, you've probably encountered it a time or two. Perhaps you're starting to see an opening where there used to be a solid wall. There are scary things on the other side of that wall, and there are also beautiful, powerful, and magical things—things that once seen cannot be unseen and will permanently change your ideas about the world and how it works.

I cannot tell you to open the door. Maybe you're not interested in deeper practice or you don't feel ready for it... but when are any of us really ready for an Otherworldly experience? Maybe you're afraid of the monsters that live in the depths. Your fears may be overblown, but they aren't groundless.

And yet, here is the door waiting to be opened.

13

PAGANS CHOP WOOD AND CARRY WATER TOO

OUR BUDDHIST FRIENDS HAVE a saying: "Before enlightenment, we chop wood and carry water. After enlightenment, we chop wood and carry water." This saying is as true for Pagans and polytheists as it is for Buddhists. Our encounters with the gods are some of the deepest, most meaningful, and most real experiences of our lives. Our magic reinforces the idea that there's more to the world than what can be dissected, measured, and catalogued. Our deeper journeys lead us to discoveries that will be helpful for those who come after us for generations to come.

My first book, *The Path of Paganism*, presented a rational argument for Paganism and a rebuttal of both the materialistic and fundamentalist worldviews that are so prevalent in our wider society. This book builds on that foundation and provides a framework for living a deeply spiritual and religious life. This is the path I've followed over the past several years. It's been very helpful to me, and I'm happier because of it.

However, we still have to pay rent and buy groceries. We still have to take our children to school and occasionally to the doctor. We still have to plan for a day when we may be sick and unable to fully care for ourselves. Even the most devout polytheists and most powerful magicians among us still have to chop wood and carry water.

The mundane presents several challenges for us, the biggest of which is finding time to do all the everyday things we have to do and still do the spiritual things we are called to do. Some tasks can be handled with ordinary time management skills: planning, scheduling, prioritization, and communicating and working with others (so you don't have to do it all yourself).

An often-overlooked practice is maintaining optionality: making decisions when you need to and not before (but don't mistake this for procrastination). The longer you can wait to make a decision, the more information you'll have, which increases the chance that you'll make the best decision and decreases the chance that you'll have to change directions and do something over again. For those of us who like to have detailed plans worked out well in advance, this isn't comfortable. But over the long term, it minimizes errors and helps us get more done.

Good work habits (with both our mundane and spiritual work) help us make effective use of our time, but sadly, it appears that the time turners from the Harry Potter world do not actually exist. Ever and always there are twenty-four hours in a day, and we need some for sleep and some for relaxation and play. At some point, doing more of one thing means doing less of something else. I watch very little television and don't read much fiction anymore. I exercise regularly (and I highly recommend it), but my days of devoting hours and hours each week to athletic training are behind me. I also don't have children. My wife and I chose to not have children because we didn't want to be parents, not because we wanted to spend our time on other matters. The fact remains that if I did have children, I'd have to make time for them.

None of these decisions and choices are "bad." None of these things are somehow less important. I probably should make time to read more fiction—good novels have been inspiring at various times in my life, and they could be again. But ever and always there are twenty-four hours in a day: some must be spent chopping wood and carrying water. Spend the rest mindfully.

HOW YOU MAKE A LIVING AND HOW YOU MAKE A LIFE ARE TWO DIFFERENT THINGS

When I first discovered Paganism, I was thrilled. I started reading and studying and practicing as much as I could. Before too long though, I backed away. One of the main reasons was the realization that I couldn't make a living being a witch or a Pagan priest. I thought I needed to "follow my bliss," and since nothing blissful would pay the bills, my true calling just had to be somewhere else. It wasn't.

Being a Druid and a priest is my true calling. I make a pittance from my writing and virtually nothing from teaching and consulting, so I pay the bills by working a day job as an engineer. Yes, it limits the time I can put into my spiritual work, and it severely limits any time for non-religious hobbies, but it works for me. There are advantages to this approach. It lets me keep my religion as religion and not as the way I make a living. I can write what I'm called to write; if it's not popular, I don't have to worry about how I'm going to eat this month. Mainly, I don't have to worry about my religion becoming a job, chore, or something I do because I have to. I'm still a long way from retirement, but I can see it from here. My hope (and plan) is to someday retire from my engineering job and become a full time Druid. If I'm able to do that, I'll have to find a new arrangement. For now, I'm happy to keep my paying work and my sacred work separate.

You will have to find your own balance. Don't fall into the trap of assuming how you make a living and how you make your life have to be the same thing.

EPILOGUE:
AN INVITATION
TO A JOURNEY

THERE ARE TIMES WHEN I'm envious of established religions. My wife is a Methodist. When we moved to North Texas in 2002, she had her choice of three Methodist churches in our suburban town and another twenty or so in our county. I drive thirty miles one way to be a part of Denton CUUPS and the Denton Unitarian Universalist Fellowship. There's now an ADF grove in the Dallas–Fort Worth area, but it's in Arlington, a sixty-mile one-way drive.

But more than a church, coven, or grove of your choice nearby, I'm envious of the established religions' infrastructure and resources, a result of two thousand years of unbroken heritage, with priesthoods, religious orders, seminaries, monasteries, and more. Huge chunks of our Pagan heritage were destroyed centuries ago. Although Pagans are rebuilding our heritage and are starting to build infrastructure, we're decades and probably centuries away from anything approaching what our ancestors in ancient Egypt or Greece or Ireland had.

We aren't operating in a vacuum. Druidry has three hundred years of heritage, though much of that is non-religious. Wicca has about eighty, and traditional witchcraft more…perhaps much more. Regardless of the exact numbers, we have more than what the current generation of Pagan elders had when they started, and they had more than the Pagans of the early twentieth century.

For the kind of ancestral, devotional, ecstatic, oracular, magical, public, Pagan polytheism that I practice and that I've discussed in this book, there is very little. Some of what our ancestors did can be found through scholarly research, but much cannot. The Druids left no written records, and what little the Romans and others wrote about them is filled with cultural bias. We know a little more about the Norse, and more still about the religions of the Eastern Mediterranean, but we have only a fraction of what once existed. And in any case, I'm not looking to rebuild Iron Age religions—I'm looking to build a contemporary religion for this place and this time.

I'm envious, but I'm not despairing. We can do this. Our gods will tell us what they want. Our ancestors will inspire us. The land itself will teach us, if we pay attention.

It requires courage, to choose a path outside the mainstream. It requires dedication, to take on tasks our Christian and atheist neighbors say are pointless. It requires perseverance, to keep going when things get difficult and when the results we want don't come quickly.

And for some of us, it requires the willingness to venture into places where there are no maps—places where no one (or at least, no one from our tribes) has been in a thousand years or more. It requires being open to spiritual experiences that the mainstream tries to rationalize away, and then examining them to see what we can learn, and what we can do to build robust religious and spiritual traditions from them. It requires taking good notes, drawing maps, and leaving signposts, so those who come after us can pick up where we left off.

I've been doing this work for the past several years, as have some local Pagan friends and co-religionists … as have various other polytheists, magicians, and mystics around the world. We don't all agree on everything, and that's fine. We serve our gods and our communities in the ways we believe are best, and then write and talk about what we do. We learn from each other: sometimes we learn what works well, other times what not to do. Slowly and gradually, we are building a collection of ancestral, devotional, ecstatic, oracular, magical, public, Pagan polytheisms worthy of our gods and ancestors.

This is the mission of *Paganism In Depth*. It's a guidebook to going deeper into the forest, higher up the mountain, and further out to sea. It's an invitation to join this sacred work, to go where there are no maps, to find your way through careful practice and intuition and pure luck, and then to draw a map for those who come after you.

Now that you've finished the book, you may be wondering what you should do next. This journey is not easy; not everyone wants to do it, and not everyone can do it. The decision is yours and yours alone.

As for me, I can't imagine doing anything else.

May the blessings of the gods and ancestors be with you now and in the days to come.

BIBLIOGRAPHY
AND REFERENCES

Beckett, John. *The Path of Paganism: An Experience-Based Guide to Modern Pagan Practice.* Woodbury, MN: Llewellyn Publications, 2017.

Bonewits, Isaac. *Real Magic.* San Francisco: Weiser, 1971.

Bonvisuto, Nicole, ed. *By Blood, Bone, and Blade: A Tribute to the Morrigan.* Charleston, SC: Bibliotheca Alexandrina via Createspace, 2014.

Burkert, Walter. *Homo Necans: The Anthropology of Ancient Greek Sacrificial Ritual and Myth.* Translated by Peter Bing. Berkeley, CA: University of California Press, 1972, 1983.

Cunningham, Scott. *Earth Power.* St. Paul, MN: Llewellyn Publications, 1983.

Daimler, Morgan. *Fairies: A Guide to the Celtic Fair Folk*. Winchester, UK: Moon Books, 2017.

———. "The Goblin Market." *Living Liminally*. 14 July 2016. http://lairbhan.blogspot.com/2016/07/the-goblin-market.html.

Derks, Richard, ed. *Hoofprints in the Wildwood: A Devotional for the Horned Lord*. Mooresville, NC: Lulu Enterprises, 2011.

Emerson, Ralph Waldo. "The Method of Nature." Boston, MA: Samuel G. Simpkins, 1841.

Evans-Wentz, Walter Yeeling. *The Fairy-Faith in Celtic Countries* (1911). *Sacred-Texts.com*, 2004. http://www.sacred-texts.com/neu/celt/ffcc/.

Geggle, Laura. "How Often Do Ice Ages Happen?" *LiveScience*, 2017. https://www.livescience.com/58407-how-often-do-ice-ages-happen.html.

Horgan, John. "Is Scientific Materialism 'Almost Certainly False'?" Scientific American, 30 January 2013. https://blogs.scientificamerican.com/cross-check/is-scientific-materialism-almost-certainly-false/.

Iamblichus. *De Mysteriis* [On the Mysteries]. Translated by Emma C. Clarke, John M. Dillion, and Jackson P. Hershbell. Atlanta, GA: The Society of Biblical Literature, 2003.

Josephson-Storm, Jason. *The Myth of Disenchantment: Magic, Modernity and the Birth of the Human Sciences*. Chicago, IL: The University of Chicago Press, 2017.

Mental Health Foundation. "Hearing Voices" (2018). https://www.mentalhealth.org.uk/a-to-z/h/hearing-voices.

Myers, Brendan. *The Earth, The Gods and The Soul: A History of Pagan Philosophy from the Iron Age to the 21st Century.* Winchester, UK: Moon Books, 2013.

"New U.S. Marathons and Halfs Report Reveals Participation Is Declining." *Competitor Running.* 20 June 2017. http://running .competitor.com/2017/06/news/new-report-2016-marathon -half-participation_165419.

Orr, Emma Restall. *The Wakeful World: Animism, Mind, and the Self in Nature.* Winchester, UK: Moon Books, 2012.

Polson, Willow. *The Veil's Edge: Exploring the Boundaries of Magic.* New York: Citadel Press, 2003.

Poseidonides, Terentios. *Depth of Praise: A Poseidon Devotional.* Charleston, SC: CreateSpace, 2016.

Ratcliffe, R.G. "Strayhorn Under Fire for Religion Litmus Test." *Houston Chronicle,* 2004. http://www.chron.com/news /houston-texas/article/Strayhorn-under-fire-for-religion-litmus -test-1971581.php.

"Routine Day." *His Holiness The 14th Dalai Lama of Tibet.* https://www.dalailama.com/the-dalai-lama/biography -and-daily-life/a-routine-day.

Sannion, ed. *Bearing Torches: A Devotional Anthology for Hekate.* Charleston, SC: Bibliotheca Alexandrina via Createspace, 2009.

Sapiro, John. "You are swimming in it; your daughter is drowning." https://johnsapiro.com/2015/06/30/you-are-swimming-in-it -your-daughter-is-drowning/.

Thomas, Kirk S. *Sacred Gifts: Reciprocity and the Gods.* Tucson, AZ: ADF Publishing, 2015.

Thrax, Theanos. "Religious Regard." *Thracian Exodus*. 14 May 2015. https://thracianexodus.wordpress.com/2015/05/14/religious-regard/.

"The Hymns of Orpheus." Translated by Thomas Taylor (1792). *Internet Sacred Text Archive*. http://www.sacred-texts.com /cla/hoo/index.htm.

White, Gordon. *The Chaos Protocols: Magical Techniques for Navigating the New Economic Reality*. Woodbury, MN: Llewellyn Publications, 2016.

Yeats, William Butler. *The Celtic Twilight* (1902). *Sacred-Texts.com*, 2001. http://www.sacred-texts.com/neu/yeats/twi/index.htm.

TO WRITE THE AUTHOR

If you wish to contact the author or would like more information about this book, please write to the author in care of Llewellyn Worldwide, and we will forward your request. Both the author and the publisher appreciate hearing from you and learning of your enjoyment of this book and how it has helped you. Llewellyn Worldwide cannot guarantee that every letter written to the author can be answered, but all will be forwarded. Please write to:

John Beckett
℅ Llewellyn Worldwide
2143 Wooddale Drive
Woodbury, MN 55125-2989

Please enclose a self-addressed stamped envelope for reply,
or $1.00 to cover costs. If outside the USA, enclose
an international postal reply coupon.

Many of Llewellyn's authors have websites with additional information and resources. For more information, please visit www.llewellyn.com.

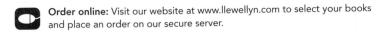